The Changing Face
of the Priesthood

A Reflection on the Priest's Crisis of Soul

Donald B. Cozzens

A Liturgical Press Book

THE LITURGICAL PRESS
Collegeville, Minnesota

2   3   4   5   6   7   8

Library of Congress Cataloging-in-Publication Data

Cozzens, Donald B.
      The changing face of the priesthood / Donald B. Cozzens.
          p.   cm.
      Includes bibliographical references and index.
      ISBN 0-8146-2504-5 (alk. paper)
      1. Priesthood.   2. Catholic Church—Clergy.   I. Title.
BX1912.C72   2000
262'.142—dc21
                                                                                99-34368
                                                                                    CIP

To the memory of my father,

Bernard A. Cozzens

1911–1984,

and

to my mother,

Florence D. Cozzens

Contents

Acknowledgments

This reflection on the priesthood developed over the last two decades. The main body of research on Chapters 4 and 5, for example, which examine the priesthood from the perspective of Freudian and Jungian psychology, was completed while I was teaching psychology and theology at Ursuline College in Cleveland from 1981 to 1989. I am grateful to the Ursuline College Library staff, especially the library's director, Betsey Belkin, for their assistance.

My early insights into the challenges facing priests in the postconciliar era were confirmed through my work with priests as spiritual director and counselor. The courage and goodness of the men who sought me out strengthened my own spiritual life. Later, for more than a half dozen years, I ministered to priests as vicar for clergy and religious in the Diocese of Cleveland. It was during this period of my priesthood that I was exposed almost daily to both the pain and the privilege of priestly life. Serving my brother priests was a humbling experience. I came to know their virtues, struggles, and failures. A few bore the marks of serious spiritual wounds and faults. Almost all were good and brave men whose inner battles often went unnoticed even by their families and close friends. Each of the men with whom I worked as vicar taught me something. I thank them.

Several congregations of women religious, through friendship and graced conversation, led me to see a profound truth: that an intimate connection exists between spiritual vitality and sound human development. They modeled lives of passionate commitment and integrated celibacy. Along the way, they helped me to contend with the dualism inherent in many of the traditional Christian spiritualities. These women, especially the writers and contemplatives among them, stretched my intellectual life through stimulating conversations that in turn shaped my reading and study. This book would be quite different without the grace and truth of their friendship. For their friendship and support, I am indebted to the Carmelite Nuns of Baltimore and Cleveland, the Dominican Sisters of Akron, the Ursuline Sisters of Cleveland, the Sisters of the Humility of Mary of Villa Maria, Pennsylvania, and the Vincentian Sisters of Charity of Cleveland.

For more than a decade now I have found friendship, laughter, and good conversation in the Saturday morning sessions of the "coffee house theologians" at Cleveland's Shaker Square. Many of the ideas discussed here were tested and debated with these faithful colleagues. They include Joseph Foley, Mary Jo Lackamp, William Laufer, Katie Leonhardy, Patricia Masterson, Margaret McIntyre, Charles Murray, Joan Panke, Gerard Sheehan, Nancy Taylor, Guy and Rita Marie Thellian, Robert Toth, Patricia Walsh, and Jeanne Yackly. For their minds and hearts, I give thanks.

My special appreciation goes to Colette Ackerman, O.C.D., James Bacik, Norman Douglas, Peter Fagan, Patrick Gibbons, Mary Catherine Hilkert, O.P., Frank McNulty, David Murphy, William and Emmy Lou Plato, Robert Toth, Ned Weist, and Mark Woyshville for their readiness to read the text in manuscript form. Their insights and good judgment strengthened the final product. I also am indebted to Thomas Cozzens, James Cozzens, Maryellen Dombek, James Finley, Conrad Gromada, Joseph Healy, M.M., Richard Hofacker, Kilian Hufgard, O.S.U., Mary Anne Kasavich, John and Elaine Lotto, Bob and Skip Meadows, Paul and Kathy Michalec, Steve and Debbie Michalec, Ted and Doris Schaetzle, Janet Schlichting, O.P., William Shannon, Mary Rose Sullivan, Melannie Svoboda, S.N.D., and Robert Wicks for their encouragement and, in some cases, their gentle prodding to see this project through to its completion. Frank and Laurie Mellion and Dick and Molly Trafas offered hospitality and quiet, ideal settings for writing.

My thanks to Bertha Popovic, my administrative secretary, and to Mary Collingwood, my graduate assistant, for invaluable assistance, especially with the final stages of writing and editing. They and Alan Rome, the Saint Mary Seminary librarian, responded with competence and understanding to my many requests. I gratefully acknowledge the guidance and encouragement of Mark Twomey, managing editor of The Liturgical Press, and the keen judgment of Peter Dwyer, marketing manager.

Donald Bernard Cozzens
Cleveland, Ohio

Introduction

Heavy, fortress-like doors opened slowly and I passed under the vaulted entrance to Cleveland's Saint Mary Seminary. I moved into a womb of monastic arches and chambers that promised to form me afresh and to carry me to birth as a priest. The seminary narthex held just enough light for me to find a place on a padded medieval bench placed against a cream stucco wall. It was early in the summer of 1957 and just a few weeks had passed since my graduation from high school. Applying for admission to the seminary required little reflection for me; I had wanted to be a priest for as long as I could remember. The priesthood of my childhood and youth, the only priesthood I knew, had but one face then, a face that defined the role of the priest for some four hundred years. I had no suspicion just how significantly the face of the priesthood was about to change.

Clearly, the priesthood to which my classmates and I felt called has changed dramatically since our ordination in 1965. Four years earlier we began our formal study of theology just as Pope John XXIII surprised the Catholic world with his call for an ecumenical council. Even as seminarians we felt the shaking of the priesthood's foundations. The priesthood we anticipated with such clarity now seemed somewhat out of focus. The very face of the priesthood—the external cues and customs, the internal hallmarks of identity and function—seemed to be changing, or better, evolving as we arrived at our first parish assignments. A generation later, the face of the priesthood continues to reveal new contours, fascinating features, and, sadly, some tragic blemishes.

The stirring breezes that greeted our first years of priestly ministry steadily gained power until reaching near-gale force. In spite of its power, most of us felt it was a benign storm, carrying in its passion a promise of a renewed Church committed to bringing the freedom and salvation of the gospel to the corners of our modern world. Aware of the historic moment that gripped the Church, we studied the documents of the Second Vatican Council with considerable excitement. As the vision of the council became ever clearer, the cultic, preconciliar model of priesthood entered into a creative balance with the servant-leader model. The clear identity, the unquestioned status, the exalted privilege—features that helped priests deal with the sacrifices and crosses inherent to their vocation—began to blur. For some priests, the council's emphasis on the dignity of baptism and the universal call to holiness raised questions about the discipline of celibacy's ascendance, at least on the level of practice, over the sacrament of marriage. For this as well as other reasons, some decided they wanted out. At present, more than half of my class of twenty-one has left the active ministry, a development mirrored in many of the larger dioceses of the United States.

While I remember vividly the heavy and somber quality of my first visit to the seminary, other memories can be retrieved. The gaunt, monk-like features of the seminarian who answered the door struck me as ominous—"Wait here until Msgr. Gallagher [the seminary's spiritual director and member of the admission team] is ready to see you. . . ." Msgr. Gallagher, it turned out, knew my grandmother, Ella Brennan Cozzens, and this fortuitous reality, I thought, might enhance my chances for admission to the seminary. The interview was brief and superficial compared to the extensive and probing process in place today for admitting candidates to our seminaries.

Serving now as rector of a seminary and chair of the admissions committee, I know our decisions are supported with more information and documentation than was the case a generation ago. Letters of recommendation, psychiatric and psychological assessments, criminal records checks, standardized tests, and a series of interviews make up the ordinary drill for admission to priestly studies today. Clearly, the data that is reviewed as part of the admissions' process is considerable. The interviews and documentation are essential, of course. Yet we still struggle, looking for signs of the reality and mystery of grace as well as for indications that the candidate has the temperament and personal strength to meet the demands of priestly ministry. Is there evidence of a genuine aptitude for priesthood? Does the applicant possess the magnanimity required for the covenant commitment at the heart of priestly service? Is he spiritually mature and intellectually capable of preaching God's word with conviction and imagination? Will the candidate under consideration aspire to be a compassionate, enthusiastic servant-leader of God's people?

One of the first rules medical students hear, I am told, is to "do no harm." It should be a rule that seminarians and priests whole-heartedly embrace. There are priests today, I'm afraid, who do more harm than good. They are, thank God, relatively few; most often they are men who have become cynical and sarcastic, lonely and bitter. Baltimore priest and writer Joseph Gallagher observes in his journal *The Pain and the Privilege*, "Now that I am a priest I have a bound-less capacity for thwarting good and for turning wine into water."[1] The priestly mission demands so much more than the negative in-junction to do no harm. We're expected, at least ideally, to bring the fire and passion of God's Spirit not only to our parishes but to the world. We're to announce salvation and deliverance in Jesus the Christ. We're meant to heal souls and speak of mysteries that are too good to be true, to awaken minds and imaginations to the new order and new being that is God's gift to all.

The chapters that follow form a reflection on the state of the priesthood at the close of the twentieth century. My own years as a priest have led me to believe that ordained ministry is indeed my call-ing, "my truth" in God's mysterious plan. The reflection, obviously, is grounded in and shaped by my own experience as a priest, especially by more than a half dozen years of service as vicar for clergy in the Diocese of Cleveland and more recently as rector of our graduate seminary. These experiences have convinced me of the great good priests have done and continue to do in service with God's people. Priests, in a special sense, are themselves rumors of angels and mes-sengers of mercy. Most do far more good than harm. Yet this book is clearly more than a paean to the priesthood. It endeavors to take a long, honest look at the present state of the priesthood, not from an empirical, scientific perspective, but rather from the perspective of one priest who may well be misreading the issues and challenges facing the priesthood today. The experiences and reflections of many priests, I am quite sure, will lead them to see a different picture than the one I outline in the pages ahead.

Acknowledging that this book represents but one priest's reflec-tion on the state of the priesthood, I have tried to paint as truthful a picture as I could of the challenges and issues facing priests and the Church at the beginning of the twenty-first century. And I have tried not to blink, not to minimize or deny those aspects that are threaten-ing the integrity and mission of the ministerial priesthood as well as

---

[1]Joseph Gallagher, *The Pain and the Privilege* (New York: Image Books, 1983) 245.

those aspects of the priesthood that serve as signs of hope and seeds of new directions. The hard look which is at the core of this reflection has inevitably led me to give considerable space to issues that are, quite frankly, both difficult and painful to write about.

Some will be disturbed by what follows, others will be threatened. Perhaps such responses are inevitable when a reflection such as this includes a spiritual and psycho-sexual analysis of priests today. It may well prove particularly challenging to candidates preparing for the priesthood. To the reader who is presently in seminary formation and to those who are discerning a call to priestly service, I ask that they remember that the hard realities of which I write are part of the human condition, the result of fallible human beings and fallible human structures. The humbling grace of priestly service, should this be your vocation, will save your soul and be a blessing for the People of God.

The present state of the priesthood, of course, reflects all the ambiguities, all the heroism and fidelity, all the cowardice and weakness present throughout the Church's history. It remains a human priesthood anointed by God's grace and itself redeemed by Christ's paschal mystery. In spite of the serious challenges recorded here, I am convinced that the priesthood is at the edge of a new day following a painful yet purifying dark night. My hope is grounded in God's promise to remain ever with this holy, yet human, Church. My hope for the priesthood, in other words, is situated in my hope for the Church.

The life of a priest, I propose here, demands, second only to faith and charity, integrity and selflessness. It is a particularly difficult and trying life when priests find themselves uncomfortable with the approved ideologies under-girding their ecclesial world and when different ecclesiologies seem to fracture the common ground that united priests in ages past. Divided themselves in painful ways, they have come to understand that the Church they serve is wounded itself, yet pregnant with hope and longing to see the full face of the Christ that continues to elude them. Understanding that the external forms of priesthood which supported clericalism and a lone-ranger type of ministry no longer hold, most priests today are sustained by a purified faith in the Gospel they preach and in the undeniable presence of God's Spirit in the men, women, and children who assemble for the breaking of bread and the proclamation of the word. Now half way through my fourth decade as a priest, it's clear to me that most priests are men of high ideals and moral passion. In spite of the changing face of the priesthood, they struggle with no little courage to serve with integrity and generosity.

The present reflection focuses on the inner life of the priest, probing the conscious and unconscious workings of his soul. For the most part, it is an intra-ecclesial look at the networks of systems—personal, family, and church based—that shape and influence priests at the turn of the century. Significant areas of concern have fallen outside the scope of this reflection. These include the spectrum of human rights issues, both inside and outside the Church, the role of women in the Church, ecumenical and inter-faith challenges, the impact of globalization, and an amoral world economy. The Church's pastors and preachers cannot ignore these issues in good conscience. While recognizing that the mission of the priest extends beyond the boundaries of his parish, these and other important ministerial issues remain outside the focus of the present reflection.

In the chapters ahead, I draw upon observations from my own pastoral experience, clinical data, and theoretical models from both Freudian and Jungian psychology. In doing so, I have tried to write from my center about what matters most to me. And I write aware of Kathleen Norris' warning that "when we write from the center . . . when we write about what matters to us most, words will take us places we don't want to go. You begin to see that you will have to say things you don't want to say, that may even be dangerous to say, but are absolutely necessary."[2] While the focus here is on the ordained priesthood, those who minister in Christ's name and proclaim God's word will find their struggles chronicled in this book. It is my hope that the reflection that follows will contribute to the understanding of the challenges facing the Church at the beginning of the third millennium.

[2]Kathleen Norris, *Amazing Grace: A Vocabulary of Faith* (New York: Riverhead Books, 1998) 273.

Part I
Issues

1

Discovering an Identity

Catholics seem to imagine their clergy differently than do members of other denominations. Despite themselves and the crisis in their morale, priests are nonetheless perceived as sacraments of a world that transcends our own. They are the sacramental persons par excellence. They want to be, if one is to credit the passionate assertions of some priests, "just like everyone else." But the Catholic imagination, fully aware of the human limitations of its clergy, still imagines them as "different," as hints of what the ever-lurking God is like, as rumors of angels, as men who point to a world beyond themselves, as signals of the transcendent God.

—Andrew Greeley
The Catholic Myth

Even in our secular, postmodern culture, the collar and black suit can still rustle memories of the gentle cheerfulness and soothing presence long associated with parish priests. These men of mystery awakened in their parishioners an often unnamed but real hunger for a deeper life in the spirit, for the ecstatic union with God and others that so often followed their moments of sacramental praise and thanksgiving. They were the men who reminded their parishioners of God's scandalous, unconditional love. Through their preaching and pastoral care, they proclaimed God's mercy and the ultimate goodness of life. Icons of the Christ no longer visible, priests remained at the center of the Catholic imagination of many, if not most, Catholics.

In a 1986 address to the United States Conference of Bishops, Archbishop Daniel Pilarczyk recalled his image of the priest when he entered the seminary in 1948 at age fourteen.

The priest dealt with sacred matters in a sacred language. He was versed in the mysteries of the faith. He was holy by the mere fact of being a

3

priest. He was highly educated and wise, and had unquestioned authority in every facet of the parish. It did not matter much if he could not preach very well. The really important thing was that he could celebrate Mass.

The specifics of his personal life were shrouded in mystery. He seemed happy, and he seemed to live better than most of the parishioners. . . . To be a priest was the highest life a boy could aspire to. It meant being a real Christian, it meant being called to serve Christ and his church, it meant being respected and revered almost as Christ himself.[1]

Almost two generations later, however, the role and place of the priest in the social order of parish life remains conflicted and ambiguous. Tender of God's mercy, perhaps, but also the spokesperson for moral and doctrinal pronouncements that at times appear to rely more on the assertion of ecclesial authority than on compelling biblical or theological persuasion. While still a symbol of the saving mercy of God, the priest remained in the eyes of many an enigma, a man out of step with the lives of the people he served. A few seemed to delight in the role of moral enforcer, evoking Blake's somber verse, "And priests in black gowns, were walking their rounds, and binding with briers my joys & desires."[2] And to those outside Catholic culture, the priest continues to be seen either as an anomaly in a secular age or as an anchor for virtue and decency in a time of moral relativism. One thing seems clear—the image of the priesthood once captured in the gentle pastoring of a Father O'Malley in *The Bells of St. Mary* no longer holds.

Other images, devoid of sentimentalism, continue to surface as the priesthood strives to renew itself in light of the general renewal inspired by the Second Vatican Council.[3] Summarizing the emergence of new identities and images of the priest, James Bacik identified a number of major shifts that occurred after the council: "from pedestal to participation; from classical preacher to contemporary mystagogue; from the lone ranger style to collaborative ministry; from a monastic spirituality to a secular spirituality; from saving souls to liberating people."[4] Bacik is correct, I believe, in grounding the priest's post-conciliar search for

---

[1]Daniel Pilarczyk, "The Changing Image of the Priest," *Origins* (July 3, 1986) 140–41.

[2]William Blake, "The Garden of Love," *Songs of Innocence and of Experience* (Oxford & New York: Oxford University Press, 1970) 145.

[3]*Presbyterorum ordinis,* nos. 2, 4, 5; Lumen gentium, nos. 1, 28.

[4]See James J. Bacik, *(Toledo) Catholic Chronicle.* The *Catholic Chronicle* published a series of essays by Bacik on the morale of priests from September 29, 1989, to February 16, 1990.

identity in the shift from a cultic model of priesthood, represented in the "from" part of the dyads noted above, to more of a "servant-leader" model represented in the "to" segment of the dyads.

Pilarczyk's depiction of his boyhood image of the priest captures many of the key elements of the cultic mode: the priest as mediator between God and human beings; the provider of the sacraments; the guardian of sacred space and sacred truth. A growing number of priests, however, encouraged by the spirit and vision of John XXIII and having read and internalized the conciliar documents, have come to find a different vision shaping their ministry and redefining their identity.

Recent scholarly attention focused on the identity of the priest has clarified the basic issues and positions under-girding the present state of the question. Whether or not a consensus is emerging remains unclear.[5] The evolution from the cultic model of priesthood to the emerging models more or less accurately grouped under the servant-leader model was bound to produce considerable anxiety on the part of the priest and a certain unease on the part of both priests and laity. Thomas Rausch observes that

> the demise of the sacral model of priesthood and the substitution of the word "presider" for "priest" in reference to eucharistic leadership has contributed to a loss of identity for many priests. . . . On the other hand, it is important to avoid any suggestion that the priest is over the church or prior to the church rather than a part of it.[6]

Priests are now in the midst of discovering a deeper, more holistic identity as members of the People of God and as presbyters of the Church. The discovery, as is the case of all authentic identities, is both an achievement and an awakening. Understanding the factors at play here can facilitate both aspects of the discovery.

---

[5]See Thomas P. Rausch, "Priestly Identity: Priority of Representation and the Iconic Argument," *Worship*, vol. 73 (1999) 169–79. Rausch offers a clear and balanced summary of the present issue, considerably advancing the discussion with his analysis of the representative and sacral models of priesthood. See also Edward J. Kilmartin, "Apostolic Office: Sacrament of Christ," *Theological Studies*, vol. 36 (1975) 243–64; Avery Dulles, "Models for Ministerial Priesthood," *Origins*, vol. 29 (1990) 284–89; David N. Power, "Representing Christ in Community and Sacrament," in Donald J. Goergen, *Being a Priest Today* (Collegeville: The Liturgical Press, 1992) 97–123; Susan K. Wood, "Priestly Identity: Sacrament of the Ecclesial Community," *Worship*, vol. 69 (1995) 109–27; Denis Edwards, "Personal Symbol of Communion," in Donald B. Cozzens, *The Spirituality of the Diocesan Priest* (Collegeville: The Liturgical Press, 1997) 73–84.

[6]Rausch, "Priestly Identity," 174–75.

Bacik's commentary on the dynamic tension of role and function shaping the priest's identity question sheds considerable light on the psychic energy and courage required to negotiate the present search. Drawing on his analysis, the following illustrations reveal the considerable stress and pressures associated with the priest's search for a post-conciliar identity:

From pedestal to participation. Convinced of the fundamental dignity and basic equality of the people of God, many priests are trying to relate to their parishioners as leader-companions rather than someone exercising unquestioned authority.

> In their pastoral practice they stress the co-responsibility of all the baptized for the well-being of the church. They do more socializing with the people they serve and are willing to enter into honest dialogue with them. Discussions of common hopes and struggles form deeper bonds between clergy and laity and make clearer the limitations and faults of priests.[7]

From classical preacher to bearer of the mystery. Preaching out of the cultic model often emphasizes the truths of the faith and morally correct behavior. It tends to be both instructional and exhortatory in tone. Bacik observes that

> today many priests are not comfortable with this (cultic model) approach. They prefer to see themselves as mystagogues who help evoke a sense of the mystery in the people they serve. Their homilies are designed not to pour new knowledge and inspiration into empty minds and hearts, but rather to enable people to become more aware of the God within who calls each of us to responsible action on behalf of the kingdom.[8]

Speaking at the 1995 convention of the National Federation of Priests' Councils, Cardinal Joseph Bernardin entitled his address, "Priests: Religious Leaders, Doctors of the Soul." "The priest of Jesus Christ," Bernardin stressed, "is, first and foremost, the one who bears the Mystery of God and initiates others into it. . . . The priest is the one who bears that strange power and who leads the people of God into an ever more intimate contact with it. In carrying out this task, one is most authentically a priest."[9] The image of the priest as mystagogue is behind the metaphors that portray him as *bearer of the mystery, doctor of souls,* and *tender of the word.*

[7]Ibid., 12.
[8]Ibid., 14.
[9]Joseph Bernardin, "Priests: Religious Leaders, Doctors of the Soul," *The Priesthood Today: Presentations of the 27th Annual NFPC Convention,* San Diego, May 1–4, 1995, 8–9.

From the lone-ranger style to collaborative ministry. Focused on the priestly power to "confect" the Eucharist and "administer" the sacraments, the cultic model encourages an individualistic approach to ministry by emphasizing the priest's unique sacramental power. The servant-leader model, without denigrating the unique role of the ministerial priesthood, tends to focus on the ministerial gifts of the parish community. One of the major responsibilities of the pastor in this model is to identify parishioners with ministerial charisms, call them forth to service, and to encourage the development of their specific gifts and talents. Priest, deacon, director of religious education, director of liturgy, and youth minister form a pastoral staff that ministers to the parishioners. Collaborative ministry is particularly challenging for priests who are secure in an exclusively cultic model and identity of priesthood and who have not learned the essential skills required for such ministry.

From a monastic spirituality to a secular spirituality. For centuries the priest's spirituality has been strongly influenced by the great monastic orders and by such mendicant congregations as the Dominicans and Franciscans. Spiritual formation in seminaries, significantly shaped by Sulpician and Irish approaches, passed on spiritual ideals and practices more suited to religious living in community than to parish priests living alone or in rectories with one or two other priests.

Especially in the case of the diocesan priest, his spirituality was grounded in what was understood to be his ontological status as a priest of the Church. Because of his power to consecrate, forgive, and anoint, came the responsibility to lead a holy life worthy of his presbyteral status. While committed to holiness of life, the parish priest began to question the suitability and feasibility of the monastic-religious spiritualities in which he had been formed. The very rhythm of parochial life, the incessant demands and calls for ministry, require a spirituality that is nourished by pastoral ministry itself.[10]

Recognizing the tension inherent in the monastic model, Bacik proposes that since parish priests have more in common with the busy people they serve than with monks or religious, a spirituality that works beyond the routine of the cloister would be better suited to the priest in parish ministry. "Priests living out a type of secular spirituality allow their ministerial activities to dictate the content and rhythm of their spiritual quest."[11]

[10]See Donald B. Cozzens, "Tenders of the Word," in Donald B. Cozzens, ed., *The Spirituality of the Diocesan Priest* (Collegeville: The Liturgical Press, 1997) 42–58.
[11]James J. Bacik, *(Toledo) Catholic Chronicle,* November 10, 1989, 16.

From saving souls to liberating people. Saving souls through pastoral care and the celebration of the sacraments is the primary function of the priest from the perspective of the cultic model. Recent decades have seen that perspective expand to the point where the communal dimension to salvation has received appropriate consideration. The people of God are redeemed and saved as a *people*. Without diminishing the essential role of personal surrender to the loving plan of God required of every individual, a renewed sense of belonging to a covenant people has led to a new awareness of social sin and institutional evil. This, in turn, has evoked a keen awareness of the constitutive place that work for justice, peace, and liberation holds at the center of the Christian life. The community of faith and the social order surface as the enduring context for God's saving grace. Bacik comments:

> Priests who have accepted and assimilated the social dimension of the Gospel are not comfortable in the cultic model. . . . These priests experience added pressures and tensions if their parishioners do not accept this linkage and want to confine the clergy to church affairs.[12]

The Instruction

The issue of priestly identity received considerable attention in 1997 with the promulgation of the *Instruction on Certain Questions Regarding the Collaboration of the Non-Ordained Faithful in the Sacred Ministry of Priests*, jointly issued by eight Vatican offices with the "specific" approval of Pope John Paul II.[13] While the focus of the *Instruction* was on the sacred character of the ministry of the priest as distinct from the ministry of the common priesthood of the faithful, the document held that lay ministry, rather than flowing from baptism, is ancillary to the ministry of the ordained priesthood.

The authors of the *Instruction* feared that lay ministry was encroaching on the ministries specifically identified with the ministerial priesthood. According to the *Instruction*, the blurring of roles and identities is a factor in the drastic decline of priests and seminarians in many parts of the world and a source of confusion to both the non-ordained and ordained faithful.

---

[12]Ibid., 17.

[13]The *Instruction*, approved by John Paul II on August 13, 1997, and signed by eight heads of Vatican dicasteries on August 15, 1997, was embargoed until November 1997.

Furthermore, the document argues, the confusion has led to pastoral and liturgical abuses.[14] Not only does the *Instruction* reveal the Vatican's anxiety about the evolving identity of the ordained priest, it emphasizes the "indispensable role of the ordained priest in the life of the church."[15] This last point, if not linked with the priest's common participation with other baptized People of God, carries implications, as we shall see, for the priest's spiritual and psychological stability.

The Search

At the core of the priest's crisis of soul, then, is the search for his unfolding identity as an ordained servant of Jesus Christ. Behind and beyond issues of integrity and intimacy that shape the quality of his soul lies the lingering question of his true self as one ordained into the priesthood of the one High Priest. So fundamental is this question that it colors every aspect of his life—his very carriage and demeanor, the way he communicates and relates, the manner in which he speaks to parishioners, friends, and brother priests.

The issue of the priest's identity grips the roots of his soul and both grounds him in his ecclesial role as presbyter and inspires him to enter into the mystery of who he is becoming as one called to this unique and extraordinary path of life. As much an existential issue as a theological one, the question takes him beyond the traditional and current theologies of the priesthood. And precisely because it is so difficult to address rationally and systematically, especially in periods of intense theological fermentation, he easily puts the question aside. The press of ministry becomes a welcome distraction from the soul work demanded by the unsettling questions. While some priests deny concern about their priestly identity, most concede that the issue hangs over their heads like a storm cloud, robbing them of the confidence they once knew, rendering them awkward and self-conscious in certain parish and social situations.

In general, a certain unease and awkwardness accompanies anyone's search for identity since identity is at the same time both a constant and an evolving reality. Even though an individual experiences a

[14]Thomas O'Meara of the University of Notre Dame commented on the *Instruction:* "We've had this new model (of lay ministry) for 25 years. The pastor is not threatened or diminished—in a way he's enhanced, he has a more challenging job. But the role of the presbyter/bishop is clear and not questioned." *National Catholic Reporter,* December 5, 1997, 14.

[15]Bishop James Hoffman of Toledo, *National Catholic Reporter,* December 5, 1997, 14.

sense of ego-awareness that remains constant throughout his or her life, identity's fluid character renders it illusive and ethereal. Ultimately, of course, our true identity remains a mystery hidden in God. Both our resting in God's grace and the living out of our faith journey submerge our ego-consciousness, our surface identity, into the mystical union of our true selves in God. From this perspective, our identity remains beyond our reach. From time to time, however, we glimpse the ecstasy of divine union and experience our identity in God. But these moments of grace pass and we return to the dimension of everyday life where true identity remains hidden.

Both profoundly intimate and obviously social, the sense of one's identity touches literally every aspect of personality and serves as the filter through which pass the daily events and rhythmic patterns of life. Yet unless priests choose to wrestle with the implications of their evolving identity, the shadow of unfinished soul work drains their energy and weakens their confidence. While most priests feel a certain anxiety associated with their evolving identity, more than a few do not. They are quite at home with the cultic model and lack any inclination to join the search. Yet it is hoped that these men will see that their priestly identity is not something static in spite of the priesthood's core reality and truth in Jesus Christ.

The priest's ecclesial identity will continue to blossom just as an individual's personal identity unfolds through his or her stages of development: from childhood through adolescence, from early adulthood through late adulthood. Ultimately, the reality and mission of the priesthood, and thus its identity, remain grounded in the mystery of Jesus Christ, in the mystery of the triune God. Perhaps that truth explains why for so many priests, the identity issue dissolves when they enter into the assembly for worship and prayer. For only in the assembly of the faithful, in the midst of their sisters and brothers in Christ and the Spirit, do they fully experience their role as servant-leader and glimpse, with the rest of the faithful, the grace of their identity in the unfailing mercy and love of God.

The Dialectic of Priestly Identity

Archetypal psychology has long proposed the interesting concept of the dyad or bi-polar archetype.[16] Archetypes, ancient cultural and

---

[16]See Adolf Guggenbühl-Craig, *Power in the Helping Professions* (Dallas: Spring Publications, 1971) especially 85–101. Guggenbühl-Craig explores the shadow side, the unconscious dynamics, that put those in the helping professions at risk to do more harm than good.

social patterns ingrained in the collective unconscious, provide a kind of universal meaning and understanding for the fundamental roles that are found in every civilization. Included among the archetypal roles are such common functionaries as king, queen, teacher, sage, warrior, mother, father, shaman, and priest. Some are essentially linked to a partnering archetype, thus the term dyad archetype. Among the more obvious dyads are: the *doctor/patient; teacher/student; king/subject; priest/parishioner* archetypes.

If we think only of the superior pole of the archetype, that is, of the doctor, the teacher, the king, the priest, the dyad is broken and the negative aspects of each may take over and dominate the inner life of the soul. A physician, therefore, who fails to see that he or she remains, in a certain sense, a patient even while tending to others in need of healing has broken the archetype, and in an effort to be scientific, empirical, and objective, weakens the healing power of the therapeutic relationship. Good doctors have an inherent respect for the *physician* in each of their patients. The same negative force occurs if the inferior pole of the dyad is embraced without embracing the superior pole. For patients, too, have the power to break the doctor/patient archetype. By failing to trust their own powers of healing, by giving too much authority to the physician, they work against their own inner resources for recovery and wholeness.

Physicians and patients, on the other hand, who hold the dyad in place, who enter into a therapeutic alliance, draw out from each other energies and insights that foster correct diagnoses and treatments. Doctors revered by their patients are humble healers who have held the dyad together. When a physician breaks the dyad archetype, however, signs of arrogance and elitism are likely to surface. With the dyad broken, the physician is no longer grounded, no longer close to the earth. Ego-inflation and hubris often stifle a sense of calling or vocation.

The same may be said for the teacher/student, the king/subject, the priest/parishioner archetypes. The teachers we remember with a certain fondness and respect most likely never forgot that they were learners also and that their students were in some real sense teachers to themselves and teachers to their teachers. By protecting the dyad, teachers protected that which is holy and sacred in the educational process. The dignity of the student was reverenced and protected and the souls of both teacher and student were, at least from time to time, able to experience the transforming ecstasy of learning. Learning in such an environment becomes a communal adventure with the real possibility of leading to wisdom and compassion. With the dyad broken, however, the classroom becomes an arena for a contest of wills.

Information may be communicated, formulae memorized, but the passage to wonder and truth fails to materialize. Politicians (kings and queens) who fail to see themselves as citizens (subjects), as those who are governed, likewise break the archetype with similar consequences to the common good.

If we place the priest archetype in the dyad cluster, the dialectical dimension to his identity becomes clear. While ordained for priestly ministry, the priest remains a member of the faithful in need of ministry and community. If true to his calling, the priest evokes in his parishioners an awareness of their priestly character as baptized believers. Distinct roles are respected while the inherent mutuality of the members of a local church is allowed to flourish. The same transforming effect resulting from the unbroken teacher/student archetype takes hold of the faith community—a sense of the mystery of God's grace relentlessly shaping an assembly into a community of praise and service. The local church inches closer to a wisdom community where parishioners perceive their pastor as elder and shepherd but also as brother and friend.

The dyad, unfortunately, is easily broken by either of its polar elements. The priest may forget that as a member of the faithful he too needs to hear God's word, needs to be ministered unto. Though one who preaches, he listens with open heart to the preaching of others. Though one who blesses, he too bows his head to receive the blessing of others. Though addressed as "Father," he is nonetheless son and brother. Rupture the priest/parishioner dyad and the priest begins to relate to the parish from a distance as it were, as one set apart. Both he and the members of the local church wrestle with the nagging suspicion that something isn't as it should be.

Parishioners, in their turn, may break the dyad by idealizing their pastor. (Priests of late report this phenomenon very rarely.) In this situation, the relationship between the priest and the people of the parish takes on a cordial yet formal tone. There is clearly a good deal of politeness but not much authentic friendship. Here the hierarchical nature of the parish is pushed to the extreme while the communal dimension suffers. Should the priest try to emphasize the communal nature of the parish, he may find his efforts met with polite resistance. There is, after all, a certain comfort in knowing one's place and in clearly defined social roles. On a superficial level, a ruptured priest/parishioner dyad functions rather smoothly, but often at the price of the soul of the parish and the isolation of the pastor.

From the perspective of individual psychology, a presbyter's identity is simply that of an ordained priest. Priesthood is his truth, the individual truth discovered in responding to the call of the Church and to the call of God's spirit rising from the depths of his soul. It is his vocation. It is what he is and what he does. From the perspective of his place as *one of the faithful*, he may with little reflection understand that he is a creature of the one Creator, fashioned into God's image, led to new life through the communal, covenant waters of baptism, and drawn by powers not fully understood to further the reign of God by the proclamation of the Gospel and the service of God's people as a priest of Jesus Christ.

The priest, then, is both pastor and parishioner, both preacher and listener. Maintaining the healthy tension of this dialectic is challenging. It is made easier, however, by the priest's experience of failure and weakness, by his human limitations, by the suffering that touches everyone's life. Perhaps that is why depth of soul and extraordinary compassion are found in those priests who have borne the heat of the day. These men are ordinarily in their middle years or beyond. Decades of priestly service have tempered their spirits—they have come to treat both praise and criticism with a certain indifference. At home with themselves, they have come to terms with their own demons and have not lost heart or their nerve. Grounded in the mystery of grace, they are both men of hope and men without illusions. They have sustained the dyad and in doing so discovered their *truth*, that core of their being where the mystery of grace in the midst of the faithful, confirms in wordless and image-less silence their call to priestly service.

2

Guarding One's Integrity

One of the priest's first services
to the world is to tell the truth.

—Cardinal Suhard

Priests and bishops are torn between
their loyalties to the laity and to the Pope
and fall back on equivocations and hypocrisy.

—Charles Morris
American Catholic

The vast majority of priests prize their loyalty to the Gospel and
to the Church. They strive to be obedient to the Church and to the
word of God. Their loyalty and obedience to the Church, however,
are not without complexity. Some sense it is possible to sell their souls
in service to the Church if their obedience is not mature and under-
girded by their own integrity. Theoretically at least, priests understand
that their obedience to the Church is not to be a blind and unthinking obedience. Their challenge is to be true men of the Church and
at the same time their own person. This fidelity to Church and conscience implies a certain tension in the life of the priest. Sooner or
later, every priest struggling for personal integrity feels it. Because he
believes the Church enjoys the abiding presence and guidance of the
Spirit, he is rightly disposed to trust the integrity of its teachings. In the
pre-conciliar years, there were relatively few tensions with the institutional, teaching Church. While he knows well the central role played by
an informed and faithful conscience in the life of the Christian, sometimes his own experiences of ministry places him in conflict with church
teaching or discipline. The tension that follows is painful. So painful, in
fact, that some priests adapt an attitude of unthinking obedience and

15

loyalty simply to escape the discomfort of being in tension with the Church they love.

The late Bernard Häring, a theologian distinguished for his own integrity and fidelity, observes:

> Religious obedience has quite an exceptional dignity. In its absolute form, we owe religious obedience to God alone. But just as God's revelation comes to us only when mediated, so too, the truths of faith reach us only when mediated. The meaning of faith and the authenticity of religious obedience confront a crisis when religious authorities . . . demand all too much submission to an obscure package of doctrines.[1]

A less than adult obedience, then, may compromise a priest's integrity. Quite unwittingly he may become a "kept man," expecting to be taken care of because of his supposed loyalty and obedience to the Church.

The antidote to this compromise in integrity is the courage to think. But thinking, the priest discovered in the seminary or even earlier, can be dangerous. It may easily lead to uncertainty, and uncertainty in turn to anxiety. Sometimes priests try to escape the discomfort of anxiety by embracing in a non-thinking and non-reflective manner the doctrines, traditions, and customs of the Church. The relief is short-lived. At these moments most priests stand in the fire of the Spirit and sense the need for honest thought and hard study. They begin to read in the areas of theology, Scripture, and the human sciences. They begin to think about and reflect upon their lived experience as human beings, Christians, and priests. Turning from study and thought blocks their ability to minister as mature persons of integrity. They may preach the Gospel, but the assembly senses that they have yet to live it.

The task of achieving and maintaining integrity is often compounded by the priest's family of origin. The nature of the priest's relationship with his father and mother is often a reliable indicator of the degree of difficulty he will likely encounter in maintaining his integrity. Priests with dysfunctional family backgrounds and serious, unresolved authority issues often feel under attack by the most reasonable expectations and directives of their bishops. In these men, their subjective, misguided struggle for integrity is much more a fight against spiritual annihilation. Prescinding from these cases of family related authority issues, the priest who has suffered loss of soul through the compromise of his integrity finds his spiritual life equally compro-

---

[1]Bernard Häring, *The Virtues of an Authentic Life: A Celebration of Spiritual Maturity,* trans. Peter Heinegg (Liguori, Mo.: Liguori Publications, 1997) 158–59.

mised. Spiritual exercises become sentimental distractions that serve to quiet the disturbing eruptions of his bad conscience. The guilt of his bad conscience often goes unrecognized for, in his own eyes, he is a good priest, clearly obedient to his Church.

Priests whose compromised integrity sustains an immature pseudo-obedience tend to ask, "What can the priesthood do for me?", the banner-cry of clericalism.[2] The subservient, always docile priest, not infrequently turns out to be demanding and authoritarian. As one Milwaukee priest put it:

> The priest is very often dominated for a long period of time so that he is led to believe that whatever authority says is the voice of God. Consequently, when he finally reaches authority, he becomes very domineering and uncompromising himself. His life has been filled with so many frustrations for so many years that he better damn well get his way because this is his last chance.[3]

Some priests report feeling compromised by the very clerical system that sustains them, "a paternalistic system of salary and residence which breed dependence and inertia."[4] A subtle, yet equally sad compromise was described in the 1988 document *Reflections on the Morale of Priests,* published by the Committee on Priestly Life and Ministry of the National Conference of Catholic Bishops:

> Among some priests, there are a significant number who have settled for a part-time presence to their priesthood. Many feel they have worked hard and long to implement, or at least adjust to, the practical consequences of Vatican II. They sense that much of that effort is now being blunted or even betrayed and they elect to drop out quietly. This is particularly true of those in the 45 to 60 age group who are willing

---

[2]Raymond Hedin, *Married to the Church* (Bloomington & Indianapolis: Indiana University Press, 1995) 68.

[3]Ibid., 181.

[4]Ibid., 232. Hedin earlier observed,

> It is this once-nurturing/female church turning impersonal/male who is revealing her less attractive side more fully now that my classmates are well into the middle years of their relationship; it is this church which demands their total allegiance without offering warmth in return, still insisting that they serve her exclusively and until death without promising a comparable fidelity to them. Older priests may yet "love the church" (I heard that phrase from two of our former teachers [seminary professors]), but my classmates find it hard to love a woman/man/institution who/which has them "by the balls." It is hard for them to retain a full sense of commitment to someone who "keeps" them under control without keeping them secure and without showing much appreciation for what their commitment costs them (166).

to go through the necessary minimum of motions but whose hearts and energies are elsewhere. Many more of our priests believed in renewal, were willing to adapt, worked hard and now are just plain tired.[5]

It is easy to accuse priests who have taken leaves of absence from active ministry or those who have outright resigned from the priesthood of compromised integrity. Few priests make that uncharitable judgment. Most seem to understand that there may well be more integrity in taking some time away from priesthood than there is in simply going through the motions.

All Their Losses

Priests continue to grieve a number of losses. They have lost their innocence and the trust that for so long was simply taken for granted. The absolute confidence parents once placed in them has faded into a wary cordiality. They have lost their once unquestioned authority, their role as moral leaders and spiritual guides. They have lost their place in the hearts of at least some of their parishioners. Teenagers turn elsewhere when confused and desperate for an understanding ear. Young adults are not always comfortable in their presence. Furthermore, the crisis of confidence has crept into their own ranks. Priests don't trust one another the way they used to. Men they have known for years, unless among their closest friends, are scrutinized for signs of misconduct with minors, for behaviors that might again harm the young and further erode the confidence in which they were once held.

Lost too were brother priests whose pain and discouragement led them to resign and seek the comforting grace and intimacy of marriage. As a former vicar for clergy, I've listened to dozens of priests speak of their anguished discernment to leave and marry. Underneath the pros and cons, their love of preaching and presiding at Eucharist, I heard them speak of a battle to save their integrity. At the same time, I know of some priests who would never think of leaving, even though they do more harm than good.[6] For more than fifteen years now priests have reeled at allegation after allegation brought against Catholic clergy for sexual misconduct with teenage boys and, in some cases, with children. If their personal integrity was not at risk, their

[5]"Reflections on the Morale of Priests," *Origins,* vol. 18, no. 31 (January 12, 1989).

[6]See Charles R. Morris, *American Catholic* (New York: Times Books, 1997) 287–88. Morris reports two extreme examples of priests who failed to maintain their integrity.

corporate integrity suffered. They could take little consolation in church officials who reminded the public that boundary violations with minors was a social problem and that the percentage of priests involved in these behaviors was about the same as other professionals having regular contact with teenagers and children.[7] Is it possible, they ask, that some of their colleagues are making subtle and incremental compromises with their integrity as they attempt to explain the scandal to their parishioners?

Some priests have lost confidence in their chanceries and seminaries. Even the best of bishops and chancery staffs can be caught in the grip of institutional paralysis and denial. They sense a reluctance on the part of diocesan officials to listen to the import of their own data if the data suggests structural or policy changes that are not in harmony with traditional or current church practices. They point to the paucity of serious theological reflection among church leaders on the dearth of vocations to the priesthood and religious life. Instead, strategies for more effective recruitment by vocation directors and parish priests are discussed while Catholics are urged to pray for vocations. As important as these initiatives are, they easily distract from the hard creative and analytical thinking demanded of the present situation.[8]

Integrity and Denial

As a pilgrim people, the Church turns again and again to the Holy Spirit seeking strength and wisdom to remain faithful to its mission. Though grounded in the truth of the Spirit and guided by her wisdom, the Church as a human institution is subject to the patterns and dynamics identified by such social sciences as organizational development, systems analysis, and social psychology. To the extent that the Church ignores social patterns and organizational dynamics it risks losing sight of its pastoral mission and compromising its ecclesial integrity. Institutions and organizations, for example, that fail to take seriously their own as well as external data practice a kind of denial that is sustained by the blinding force of their own previous successes.

Social science research, for example, has discovered a strong tendency in very successful mega-organizations to deny their own data as well as external data if it points to the need for change and adaptation.

[7] Andrew M. Greeley, "How Serious Is the Problem of Sexual Abuse by Clergy?" *America*, vol. 168, no. 10 (March 20–27, 1993) 6–10.

[8] See Richard A. Schoenherr and Lawrence A. Young, *Full Pews & Empty Altars: Demographics of the Priest Shortage in United States Catholic Dioceses* (Madison, Wis.: University of Wisconsin Press, 1993).

I draw here upon the research of Harry Levinson as reported in his 1993 Award Address to the American Psychological Association. If we examine Levinson's findings from the perspective of the institutional Church, the dynamics of denial arguably present in some of the Church's reactions to such difficult issues as the graying of the clergy, parishes without resident pastors, and clergy misconduct with minors are seen in a fresh light.[9] Social science research has tracked the decline of such corporate giants as General Motors, IBM, Sears, and other major American corporations. The past success of these behemoths made the senior-level executives reluctant to take seriously their own data concerning foreign and domestic competition, consumer demands for quality, and frontier, industry-changing technology.

Executive officers tended to give in to a kind of narcissistic inflation that in turn bred disdain for competitive companies. At the same time, these same executives grew less open to directions that would take them away from structures, strategies and procedures that had proven to be extraordinarily successful in the past. Their leadership became mired in "rigid corporate cultures and cumbersome hierarchies. . . ."[10] The American corporate giants that failed to take seriously the data before them put their companies at risk and in doing so threatened the integrity of their corporate souls.

In the eyes of many priests (as well as moderate, middle of the road Catholic laity), Vatican officials and church leaders appear to be in denial of the Church's own data. The vocation crisis is cast almost exclusively as a failure to recruit and as a failure to pray for vocations. The "graying" of the priesthood is tabled out of fear of solutions that would alter long-standing church traditions and disciplines. Discussion and study about married priests and the role of women in ministry are discouraged and in some cases forbidden.

Perhaps more critical than the graying of the clergy is the growing awareness that large numbers of priests and seminarians are homosexual in orientation. The question of disproportionate numbers of homosexual priests is clearly a tricky and delicate issue, an issue we will address in Chapter 7. Yet the implications of a largely gay priesthood must be faced compassionately but candidly.[11] But as Tim Unsworth

[9]See Harry Levinson's "Why the Behemoths Fell: Psychological Roots of Corporate Failure," *American Psychologist,* vol. 49, no. 5 (May 1994) 428–36. Levinson's research into the denial patterns of major corporations sheds light on the current crisis facing the Catholic priesthood.

[10]Ibid., 428.

[11]See Tim Unsworth, *The Last Priests in America* (New York: Crossroad, 1991). Unsworth notes that

notes in *The Last Priests in America,* "Denial and secrecy are still the commonplace defenses to most sexual problems among priests, especially for homosexual priests."[12]

Richard McBrien, writing on the topic of homosexuality and the priesthood at the invitation of the editors of *Commonweal,* noted that the issue had been called to the public's attention in such diverse publications as *Atlantic Monthly, Newsweek,* and *National Catholic Reporter.* McBrien points to the implications of large numbers of gay priests and bishops in a series of questions that are both honest and fair and at the same time unsettling.[13] In November 1989, two years after McBrien's article, Andrew Greeley warned that "the Catholic Church in this country is developing a heavily homosexual priesthood."[14] Greeley flags the integrity question when he notes the Church's reluctance to address the issue of homosexual priests and the homosexual activity some of them engage in. "Church leadership is paralyzed by these phenomena. Since it has no idea how to respond to the problem it engages in denial, a psychological mechanism that screens out evidence that everyone else sees."[15] What is of interest here is that McBrien's and Greeley's articles point to a pattern of minimization if not denial on the part of church leaders. To the extent that this is the case, the Church's integrity is at issue.

There are signs, however, that the Church is reasserting its institutional integrity by the decidedly different manner in which it has dealt with cases of sexual abuse in recent times. In June 1998, Bishop Keith Symons of Palm Beach, Florida, resigned after allegations surfaced that he had molested five young men in three different parishes in the early years of his priesthood. Instead of withdrawing behind

---

an NBC report on celibacy out of Chicago stated that "anywhere from 23 percent to 58 percent" of the Catholic clergy have a homosexual orientation. A newly ordained priest from a large, multidiocesan seminary believes that at least half his classmates were gay, and a gay Catholic layman, who frequents gay bars in his city stated, "I just can't go into a gay bar without meeting at least one priest. . . . I'm told that the diocese punishes its diocesan priests if they're seen in a gay bar. That's terribly ironic since some of the ones meting out the punishments are gay themselves." A. W. Richard Sipe's estimate is that by the year 2010, if the present trend continues, the majoritiy of the clergy will be homosexual (248).

[12]Ibid.

[13]Richard P. McBrien, "Homosexuality and the Priesthood: Questions We Can't Keep in the Closet," *Commonweal* (June 19, 1987) 380–83.

[14]Andrew M. Greeley, *National Catholic Reporter* (November 10, 1989) 13.

[15]Ibid.

carefully crafted statements from diocesan officials, Bishop Symons acknowledged the veracity of the reports, expressed his apologies to the men now in their adult years that he abused as boys, and urged them to accept the Church's offer to provide spiritual and therapeutic counseling. He also asked for prayers. Bishop Robert Lynch of St. Petersburg, Florida, appointed by the Vatican as administrator of Bishop Symons' diocese, was applauded in a local editorial for his candor and pastoral sensitivity.[16] Also, in what has been called an "extraordinary step," Cristoph Cardinal Shonborn, archbishop of Vienna, has acknowledged that charges of sexual misconduct with seminarians leveled against his predecessor, Hans Hermann Cardinal Groer, were true and proceeded to publicly apologize for the actions of the former archbishop.[17]

Conclusion

Priests continue to face their own integrity issues. Most do so with considerable moral courage. Some have blinked. They become less candid when asked their opinion. They know what their bishops want to hear; they know what people want to hear. Their failures are clearly less blatant than obvious infidelity to the Gospel, to what is clearly sinful and wrong. Yet these compromises shrink the soul of the priest, limit his effectiveness as a man of God and preacher of God's word. They rob him of the joy and freedom that allow his ministry to ring true, to reflect the integrity of soul that quietly validates his vocation as priest and pastor. These and similar seemingly insignificant infidelities may result in little discomfort to his conscience, but they work their own way into the deeper levels of soul. Here they tend to germinate into a chronic state of unrest and disease that the priest experiences as existential guilt and anxiety—telling signs of compromised integrity.

Sooner or later, however, to be human is to find oneself in a major quandary of conscience that in and by itself may determine one's fundamental integrity; that may define the quality of one's soul. Fidelity to the minor, everyday tests to one's integrity is likely to determine how one responds when faced with these significant "moments of truth." Both individual priests and the Church itself, then, must struggle to sustain their integrity. Certainly, as noted above, large numbers of priests faced a crisis of integrity following the publication of *Humanae vitae* in

[16] *New York Times,* June 3, 1998, A 12 and June 4, 1998, A 14.

[17] Alessandra Stanley, "Pope in Austria to Heal a Troubled Church," *New York Times,* June 20, 1998, A 4.

July 1968. Having listened to the stories of their parishioners, they knew firsthand the pain and anguish of couples struggling to comprehend the church's teaching on artificial birth control. For many priests it was their first, major crisis of soul, the first testing of their pastoral conscience.

Since *Humanae vitae*, there have been other Vatican decrees and declarations which placed priests between official church positions and teachings and the reality of their parishioners' lives and the insights of their own pastoral experience. In that space they stand in the fire of testing and purification. Great numbers of priests are indeed honest with themselves. They turn to prayer, study, and serious reflection. In that space they often become true men of God. Their faith and integrity, their responsibility and courage, no doubt, give glory to God.

3

Loving as a Celibate

There is no way toward divine love
except through the discovery
of human intimacy and community.

—Thomas Moore
Care of the Soul

Before coming to my present ministry as a seminary rector, I served as vicar for priests in a large mid-western diocese. Priests taking leaves of absence or resigning outright from the priesthood ordinarily met with me to discuss such things as how the parish would be informed, health coverage, retirement benefits, help in finding employment, and, of course, the canonical implications of their decisions. In almost all cases, the decision to resign or request a leave of absence had been made and confirmed. There was little in the way of counseling these men; most had talked to a counselor, discussed their decision at considerable length with a spiritual director, and passed long evenings confiding in trusted friends. The priest sitting in my office was making one of the most critical decisions of his life. Whatever was to follow, his soul and destiny would be freshly shaped by his withdrawal from active ministry. Sometimes he demonstrated the peace that follows a soul-wrenching decision. Others showed considerable anxiety and gave me a glimpse of the wounds that probably were factors in their decision. Few expressed anger at the Church, a pastor, or at unforgiving parishioners. Not one of the priests that spoke to me mentioned a loss of faith. Most were faithful to prayer and not a few enjoyed reputations as outstanding preachers and pastors. Many did, however, speak of loneliness and a desire for intimacy that seemed incompatible with the culture of celibacy. We both understood that his leaving would be seen by many as incomprehensible, and by some as a betrayal of trust at best and an act of infidelity at worst. I found these meetings both poignant and muted. We spoke in the softened tones heard in funeral homes. The atmosphere was charged with a certain sobriety—and a penetrating sadness.

After having met with a number of priests as they left active ministry, I began asking, "What will you miss most about your years as a priest?" Often the answer required no reflection whatsoever. "I will miss preaching and presiding at Mass." When I heard such responses I knew the core of his truth was rooted in the priesthood, but as far as he could discern, not a celibate priesthood. For the priest on the way out, his sadness was mitigated by a sense of peace and freedom, and the hope that what was missing in his soul might soon be realized. My own sadness, however, stayed with me for days.

Questions that not even the priest in the process of leaving could answer refused to be quieted. Was the decision made in faith? Did the priest give enough room in his ruminations for vocation's mystery and paradox? Did he understand that as he lay down one cross, he would surely pick up another? Did he understand that his soul's hunger for intimacy was not incompatible with celibacy? That intimate friendship, though difficult, was part of the divine plan for him? Did he think that falling in love was a clear indication that he was called to marriage or that he could only be fulfilled through a fully expressed sexual life with a beloved?

I raised as many of these questions as I could with the priests who met with me before leaving. Their answers, not surprisingly, were often different from mine. From time to time, one or another would have his own questions: "Isn't it possible that God is calling me both to the sacrament of orders *and* the sacrament of marriage?" And sometimes, "Is this decision, that feels so right, right for me in God's eyes?" There would be moments of clarity and insight in future years that would lead him to understand if the decision made long ago was indeed of God's spirit. But for the present, in spite of residual doubt and confusion, he was sustained in the hope that his discernment was honest and that he was being led by God's spirit. Sometimes as these good men left my office we embraced.

What was missing in the lives of these men choosing to leave the active ministry? And what was missing in the lives of many other priests who, while not leaving the priesthood, showed such clear signs of unhappiness and rancor? What is missing for many priests, I believe, is the experience of union, the intimacy of a holy communion with a few good friends. By itself, without deep and authentic human friendship, their intimacy with God made experiential through prayer, sacraments, and devotional practices leaves their spirits slightly out of balance. Over time, some come to understand that their love for God is actually deepened and strengthened by celibate, intimate friendships with others—friendships that go beyond their ministerial love for parishioners as parishioners.

The Triumph of the Therapeutic

I have learned a few things accompanying brother priests as they transitioned out of the priesthood. The lessons confirmed what I had discovered earlier when priests came to see me for spiritual direction. No matter how disciplined the prayer life, no matter how committed the ministry, the priest's human development was a critical factor in his efforts to discover wholeness, meaning, and fulfillment—especially if he was to discover the gift of soul that appeared just beyond his reach: the gift of intimacy. The power and transcendent glory of married intimacy can never be minimized or disparaged, but fully half the world's population, it would seem, is not married. Children and teenagers, widows and widowers, singles and separated, vowed religious and priests are called to live in the image of the triune God, who is relationality and communion itself. The God who desires that all of the human family might dwell in loving communion and intimacy, certainly wills the spiritual and human fulfillment of the celibate priest, even when the discipline of the Church prohibits him from entering into the sacrament of marriage. Over the years, I suspect that some priests who left for the sacramental intimacy of marriage discovered too late that they were more isolated and lonely in the very state that promised them deliverance. This desire for union, it appears, is especially dangerous in the kind of therapeutic age that marks the last half of the twentieth century and appears to be shaping the first decades of the twenty-first.

In his important book *The Triumph of the Therapeutic,* Philip Rieff captured a major cultural theme of the last five decades of the twentieth century.[1] Therapy's triumph in an age of radical individualism has enriched our lives in numerous ways. Almost every facet of our lives has been touched, and in many cases, reshaped by the therapeutic mindset. Thanks to psychology's therapeutic focus we understand

[1] See Philip Rieff, *The Triumph of the Therapeutic* (New York: Harper Torchbooks, 1968).

better the draculean dynamics of addiction, the Byzantine twists of human motivation, and the complexity of sibling and parental ties. Where moralistic approaches predominated in past generations when society was confronted with antisocial behaviors, we now observe more compassionate and enlightened attempts to deal with destructive behavior. Both the individual and social fabric of life have benefited from psychology's ascendancy and the triumph of the therapeutic mindset. A closer look at the triumph of the therapeutic, however, reveals a triumph that is, in some cases, anything but therapeutic for the soul. The shadow side of therapy's triumph, not surprisingly, overlooks the emptying of self that is essential for authentic, graced human intimacy.

In the therapeutic world of psychology, what is good for the personality and soul of an individual becomes an entitlement one is free to pursue directly and with all the energy one can muster. In fact, one is not only free to pursue it, one has a responsibility to pursue it, and so we see countless people declare that they will settle for nothing less than the good life: a life of happiness, relative ease, and the joy of intimacy and love. And the pursuit of these goods is direct and focused. From the perspective of social science, that is, from a rational point of view, there is a certain logic here. If something is good and noble, beneficial and even essential, one would be foolish not to set out on a holy quest to obtain it. It seems that our therapeutic culture has not yet discovered the paradox of the Gospel: *some things are achieved only when they are surrendered. Happiness follows the forgetting of one's desire to be happy and living in such a way as to foster the happiness of others. Holiness follows the desire to live in harmony with God's will in selfless praise and thanksgiving. It is best pursued indirectly. Intimacy follows when one trusts that it will come once it is not directly pursued.* For like so many of life's true blessings, intimacy is primarily gift. One prepares oneself through prayer and right living—and one waits. Willfully seek intimacy and it will elude you. Willfully seek fulfillment and you will remain unfulfilled. Willfully seek holiness and you will encounter spiritual danger.

There are, of course, skills that can be acquired to facilitate relationships and even the attainment of intimacy and union, but they are at best tillers of the soil. Intimacy, like all things that really matter, is a gift of the spirit that cannot be fully earned or merited by one's singular efforts. Priests, no less than others, can easily forget this. A priest whose intimacy needs are woefully unmet may listen to the wrong voice and set out in search of what is already potentially in his heart.

Intimacy and Transcendence

At some point in their spiritual journey, priests are likely to discover two dimensions of desire that inevitably lead the soul to God: intimacy and transcendence. This desire for intimacy and transcendence, I believe, is universal. If left unfulfilled, not only is the path to God obstructed but also grave spiritual and psychological harm descends upon the frustrated seeker.

Both terms, unfortunately, are troublesome. The adjective form of *intimacy*, "intimate," has become a pseudonym for sexual relations ("I was intimate with my fiancée"). My use of the term in connection with celibate relationships excludes this connotation. *Transcendence* is perhaps even more problematic. While it holds an honored place in the lexicons of philosophy, literature, theology, and psychology, it carries an esoteric, academic ring to it. Each of these disciplines has its own understanding of the term. I use intimacy and transcendence here in a phenomenological sense, as the experience of union with another in the case of intimacy and union with creation in the case of transcendence.

We experience intimacy with another when we are able to stand before another without our usual defenses and masks, vulnerable and yet trusting. We not only find ourselves free to share our deepest fears and anxieties, we are able to reveal what is even more personal, our deepest ideals and dreams, the noblest thoughts of our souls. In these moments of union, there is no fear, no anxiety. It is important to remember, particularly for celibate clergy, that this kind of sacred union is not the exclusive domain of married love, although the very structure and state of married love is rightly understood as *the* religious and social symbol of intimate union. Married or single, young or old, individuals need a few people in their lives who are or are capable of becoming soul-mates.

Transcendence, we have seen, remains fuzzy even if we understand the context in which it is used. I use the term here to describe those elusive moments in which we experience, literally, an unspeakable, harmonious, liberating union with creation. The most common example, perhaps, is the feeling of awe and wonder that comes over an individual experiencing a panorama of stars on a clear, cloudless night. One feels both infinitely small as she experiences the vastness of the universe and yet significant, as a part of it, in communion with it. The present interest in meditation, contemplative prayer, and various "spiritualities" reveals the soul's desire for transcendent experience. The soul, I am proposing, was created for such experiences.

The ritual, symbolic richness of the sacramental life of the Church, to a great extent, meets the human need for transcendence. When the word of God is preached and heard in the power of the spirit, time ceases as the assembly tastes the glory of God's presence and mercy. When secular ritual and the performing arts, in particular, reflect with creativity and authenticity the goodness of the human spirit, audiences become anonymous communities, anointed by the same "sacrament" of transcendence. Deprived of these moments of transcendence, however, the soul turns to pseudo or plastic ones. I have felt for some time that the abuse of alcohol and other mind-altering chemicals is, at least to a degree, an attempt to meet the soul's frustrated desire for transcendence. Sooner or later, the ordinary experience of clock time and two-dimensional space simply cannot be tolerated. At these points in life, individuals are at risk for the addictive practices that offer temporary escape but enduring dependence.

If we understand intimacy as union with another, transcendence may be thought of as communion with creation. In both experiences, the individual loses self-consciousness as well as awareness of time and place. Yet his or her sense of being remains exquisite. Because our souls have been "programmed" for intimacy and transcendence, failure in these areas, we noted, may lead to synthetic or pseudo experiences that are the merest reflections of the real thing.

Intimacy and the Priesthood

The gift and grace of celibate intimacy is most likely to be realized in priests who are emotionally mature. Emotional maturity, in turn, serves as the bedrock for an authentic spiritual and intellectual life. Prayerfulness and thoughtfulness, in a reciprocal, sustaining dynamic, nourish the priest's soul to the point of maturity that illumines its need for deep and meaningful friendship with both priests and laity. Emotional maturity remains the underpinning of authentic spiritual maturity. From a biblical perspective Joann Wolski Conn has noted that "spiritual maturity is deep and inclusive love. It is the loving relationship to God and others born of the struggle to discern where and how God is present in the community, in ministry, in suffering, in religious and political dissension, and in one's own sinfulness. . . . Maturity is understood primarily as a matter of relationship."[2]

---

[2]Joann Wolski Conn, *Spiritual and Personal Maturity* (New York: Paulist Press, 1989) 16.

Lacking this maturity, priests stand at great risk to remain spiritually and intellectually underdeveloped. Prayers are said, but a true spirit of prayerfulness doesn't follow. Journals are consulted from time to time, but real thought and serious theological reflection require too much discipline. In this situation priests are likely to turn to whatever might distract them from the emptiness within. Frequently these men become preoccupied with possessions and money, with status and power. In spite of comforts and living quarters that often exceed those of their parents, brothers, and sisters, priests sense that something is missing in their lives, something that is fundamentally good, something to which they have a right. At its core, I'm convinced, is a desire for union, a longing for intimacy. If there are not a few truly close and intimate friends in the priest's life, he finds himself in serious danger. And his efforts to remain in spiritual union with God do not compensate for the existential anguish that grips his soul. At this point, the hunger for a romantic and sexual relationship easily becomes all encompassing.

Unmet intimacy needs, I believe, have led countless priests to think they could find true fulfillment only in marriage or, in the case of the homosexually oriented priest, in a sexually active relationship with another man. Whatever the orientation, the priest gives serious thought to leaving the priesthood in order to meet his soul's desire for union. Here we encounter one of the apparent paradoxes of celibate intimacy—one of the hallmarks of a healthy celibate priest is his capacity for honest, close friendships with both men and women, with both priests and laity.

While often complex and difficult, close friendships that are deep and committed meet a human need that even an intense spiritual life ordinarily is not able to fulfill. If the celibate intimacy with a few close friends is authentic, the priest discovers that the core of his heart remains fixed on God alone. In the quiet of his prayer, he comes to the edges of the mystery where dualism dissolves. Such graced friendship with another human being actually enhances his ability to live a healthy and holy celibate life. The deeper his love for God, the greater his capacity for human love and friendship. Conversely, the more authentic his celibate relationships are, the more central and self-defining is his love for God. Yet these waters remain dangerous. Every human relationship, especially intimate relationships, have a sexual dimension. The very given-ness of gender and human longing makes this so, and because of the demonic or negative forces evident in human sexuality, its capacity to deceive and distort, even the luminous and sacramental dimensions of human sexuality have been regarded with considerable suspicion.

Only in the last decades of the twentieth century have seminary formation programs paid serious attention to the role of psycho-sexual development in the spiritual development of their candidates. Some argue that seminary and other formation programs need to pay far more attention both to the theology of sexuality and to the relational skills that are necessary for priests and religious to lead meaningful and healthy celibate lives.[3]

A good number of priests still do not understand the necessary place of close friendships in their lives. Their Catholic imaginations have not been able to break free of the profound suspicion and mistrust that centuries of Catholic thought associated with human sexuality. If they are especially close to some individuals, they reason, it will be just a matter of time before they fall in love and leave the priesthood to marry. Should a priest come to believe that he has "fallen in love," he easily concludes that he is in the grips of a vocation crisis, and in a certain sense he is. But the real question is not whether to leave and marry, rather it is to discern if he and his beloved can commit to a celibate friendship. In other words, is he experiencing a vocation crisis or an intimacy crisis? Intimacy and marriage, while closely connected, are distinguishable realities. Often, the distinction is missed.

For the priest convinced that his truth is indeed the priesthood, crises of intimacy sometimes lead to exploitative relationships with a number of women or men. Appropriate emotional boundaries are crossed and frequently sexual boundaries as well. Confusion, loss of pastoral focus and energy, and considerable anxiety are likely to overcome the priest. The emotional and spiritual harm that befalls the woman or man involved with the priest is often considerable. Because the binding fabric of these relationships is loosely woven, without the strengthening threads of God's spirit, what passes for intimacy proves temporary and shallow. The relationship betrays itself as a tissue union of mutual need. Some priests, sensing the difficulties and challenges of honest celibate relationships, are drawn to pornography and other paraphilias that inevitably lead to deeper isolation. More infrequently, but far more tragically, the priest turns to the pseudo-intimacy of sexual contact with teenagers or children.

Priests who are effective preachers and pastors understand their souls' desire for intimacy with God *and* others. The force of this desire, of course, is shaped by many complex factors: the health and character of their family life, the social and cultural mores of their

---

[3]See A. W. Richard Sipe, *A Secret World: Sexuality and the Search for Celibacy* (New York: Brunner/Mazel, 1990).

time, their psycho-sexual development, their spiritual and relational histories, as well as the quality of formation they underwent as seminarians. Understanding the deeper desires of one's soul is a daunting task for any individual. In our post-conciliar age, it appears to be particularly challenging for priests. They, like their brothers and sisters in the human family, wait in faith and hope for the gift of loving friends. For in the final analysis, intimate union with another is a gift from God. The priest's task, as is everyone's, is to be ready and capable of receiving the gift.

Transcendence and the Priesthood

Boredom descends upon most everyone, it seems, with the possible exception of the saints. The developing identity of the child and teenager, the awkwardness of finding one's place socially, the tension and turmoil inherent in the integrating of the instinctual and social dynamics of human development, explain periods of boredom in the lives of the young. How is it, though, that adults regularly find the drama and adventure of life a rather boring and tedious matter. Certainly the aftermath of original sin, the tedium of much of our work, the suffering of body and soul, the violence and injustice endemic to human society, offer some explanation for the phenomenon of ennui and boredom that come over us from time to time. The very fog of boredom seems to hide its source in a pall of endless gray. Caught in the grips of boredom, time weighs heavy on our hands, space appears flat and two-dimensional, and the very joys of life offer little satisfaction. More than a few priests, I suspect, are experiencing more than their share of boredom. For some, boredom shadows their every move and renders their world, even the world of their ministry, banal.

Chronic boredom is a symptom signaling that something is amiss on the level of soul. It announces a crisis of the soul that deserves attention and care. If one sits with his or her boredom, befriends it, so to speak, listens to it, it reveals a dearth of both intimacy and transcendence. The two, we shall see, are sides of the same coin.

In spite of the extraordinary richness and meaning inherent in priestly ministry, in spite of the transcendent dimensions of the sacramental and symbolic that characterize the priest's life, he may find little energy and vitality either in his ministry or life itself. When this is the case, the ecstatic dimension of his soul's life has been lost. It is found and reclaimed as he surrenders to the poverty of spirit that allows the transcendent elements of life to reveal new horizons and to initiate moments of ecstasy. The experience of transcendence is always ecstatic; whether encountered in quiet moments of solitude or communal celebrations of liturgy. Here there is no hint of boredom—only a timeless, wordless communion with all of reality. In fact, the loss of a sense of time and place characterize the experience of transcendence. At play, children enter into zones of transcendence and literally lose track of time and place. Leisure, the art of adult play, should have the same quality.

The same phenomenon of spirit occurs when individuals are absorbed in meaningful work. The artist, especially, experiences the purifying effects of her creative work in the self-transcending commitment required of the creative act. It is not surprising, then, that in his study of creative people, psychologist and philosopher Sigmund Koch discovered that in the act of creating "the self-disappears."[4] Koch understood that the ego-self momentarily dissolves in the ecstasy that follows upon the experience of communion with God and creation. In these sacred moments there is no ego, no conscious self to be bored, only the graced experience of being *as* being.

There is, furthermore, a certain transforming or purifying effect to authentic experiences of transcendence. Freed from the constricting forces of fear and anxiety, the soul is soothed and healed. Simone Weil, in her classic *Waiting for God*, remarked that fifteen minutes of concentrated study can purify the soul.[5] Good literature, film, and the performing arts all hold the power to lead us into zones of transcendence where our souls find refreshment and renewal. A glance at one's watch, however, is a sure sign that a film or performance (or homily) has failed to capture the soul's attention. It has failed to take us out of ordinary time and place.

While lacking the urgency of the soul's desire for intimacy, the soul's need for time outside of time, what theologians term *kairos* time, remains real and enduring. Without regular experiences of transcendence, the soul falls back on artificially created ones. At least part of alcohol's addictive power, we noted above, is its ability to effect states

[4] *New York Times*, August 14, 1996, A 16.
[5] Simone Weil, *Waiting for God*, trans. Emma Craufurd (New York: Harper Colophon, 1951). See especially the essay, "Reflections on the Right Use of School Studies with the View to the Love of God," 105–16. Weil writes,

> Something in our soul has a far more violent repugnance for true attention than the flesh has for bodily fatigue. This something is much more closely connected with evil than is the flesh. That is why every time that we really concentrate our attention, we destroy the evil in ourselves. If we concentrate with this intention, a quarter of an hour of attention is better than a great many good works (111).

of consciousness that approach the graced moments of authentic experiences of transcendence.

There is, of course, a certain kind of transcendence experienced as large crowds assemble for sporting events, parades, and rock concerts. While releasing the individual from the ennui of boredom that accompanies long periods of ordinary time (*chronos* time), these collective moments of transcendence are not always touched by the divine spark that leads the soul to gratitude and wonder.[6]

Moments of graced intimacy and transcendence come and go. As ecstatic gifts of the Spirit, they resist orchestration or manipulation. When experienced, they awaken in the heart of the priest a sense of his own poverty of spirit. What he needs most urgently as a human being can only be waited upon in faith and prayer. This receptive spirit makes fertile the soil of his soul, makes him receptive to the transforming surprises of God's spirit. While experiences of human intimacy remain conflicted and problematic in the lives of many Latin-rite priests, moments of authentic transcendence, as sheer grace, regularly rain down upon them. They dwell, after all, in a world of ritual. As ministers of the Church's sacraments, their imaginations and hearts encounter the mysterious power of God's grace. If faithful and humble, their days are often rich in moments "outside of time."

So far we have discussed the priest's need for regular experiences of intimacy and transcendence if his soul's desire for union is to be realized. The focus has been on special moments, graced moments of union with God, others, and indeed, all of creation. In moments of authentic, celibate intimacy, one is, at the same time, one with God and all of creation. When caught up in the wonder and mystery of transcendent ecstasy, the soul delights in intimate communion with

---

[6]A generation ago, Thomas Merton wrote the following about the ecstatic experience of contemplation. He describes a similar phenomenon when shortcuts are attempted in the pursuit of transcendence:

> Young people today believe that if all that is said about religion is true, if God is real, then there must be some way of experiencing that truth. And if God can be experienced, why shouldn't there be a shortcut? Someone comes along and says yes, there is a shortcut, so they try it and conclude it's an experience of God. I think we've all had the equivalent of an LSD trip. I used to get it from real coffee in the old days! All you need is a kind of high. . . . It's the kind of trip you go on when you hit choir one day, and you're really keyed up, and everything just kind of bursts into flame, the whole place is rocking.

The Springs of Contemplation: A Retreat at the Abbey of Gethsemani, ed. Jane Marie Richardson (New York: Farrar, Straus, Giroux, 1992) 99.

God's creation and at the same instant embraces all of humanity. From this perspective, experiences of intimacy and transcendence are moments of true spiritual ecstasy. In the joy of intimate friendship, the priest experiences a holy union. In the awe and wonder of a moment of transcendence, the priest experiences a holy communion. In these graced moments of union and communion, the richness and over-whelming meaning of the priesthood is beyond question. Like the prophets of old, the priest holds these epiphanies in his memory, drawing strength and comfort from them. By their very nature, ec-static moments of intimacy and transcendence are *events,* events of grace designed to transform. The transformation allows the priest and every believer to dwell in a kind of *state* of intimacy and transcendence— in a *state of grace.*

Nevertheless, loving celibately and dwelling in a state of authen-tic celibate friendship would be made easier for priests if there were more models of such loving relationships. Because they are so easily misread, it is not surprising that discretion keeps many of these rela-tionships more or less in the private realms of celibates' lives. Religious congregations, especially of women, tend to be more open and sup-portive of close celibate friendships than is the diocesan presbyterate. The greater trust and minimal competition evident in communities of religious women appear to be factors here. A glimpse at two celibate friendships, one centuries old and the other rather recent, I believe, will be enlightening.

Jordan of Saxony and Diana D'Andalo

In the early 1960s, while still a theology student, I stumbled upon a small book in the seminary library. Gerald Vann's *To Heaven with Diana!* proved to be one of a handful of books during my seminary years that spoke both to my mind and heart.[7] It would be another decade before I would begin my post-seminary work in psychology and spirituality, yet the book I read with fascination planted a life-long interest in these two closely related fields. *To Heaven with Diana!,* in spite of its unforgivable title, allowed me to break through the dual-ism that under-girded much of my seminary formation. Here was a volume that spoke with passion about the pursuit of holiness and the radical compatibility of intimate human friendship with that pursuit. Not only was celibate friendship compatible with priestly and religious

---

[7]Gerald Vann, O.P., *To Heaven with Diana!* (New York: Pantheon Books, 1960). Checking the © page, I noted that Father Vann's book enjoyed a *nihil ob-stat, imprimi potest,* and *imprimatur!*

commitment and ministry, but also Vann demonstrated that honest celibate friendship, while not without its dangers, proves to be the safer course in the long run.

Vann divides *To Heaven with Diana!* into two parts. The first is a sixty-page introduction to the extraordinary friendship between Jordan of Saxony, the second master general of the newly established Dominican Order of Preachers, and Blessed Diana D'Andalo, the first superior of Dominican nuns. Drawing on the surprising passion and profound spiritual depth of Jordan's letters to Diana (Diana's letters to Jordan were lost), Vann develops a theology of spiritual friendship remarkable for its integration of divine and human love. Jordan's and Diana's hearts remain fixed on God and their ever-deepening union with God remains the context and ground of their love and mutual commitment. Their interpersonal intimacy expands their souls' capacity for wonder and awe, for those transcendent moments of communion with the ground of their being. First and foremost Dominican disciples of Christ, their love and friendship sustain them in fidelity to God's word and to the service of their sisters and brothers.

Vann's commentary on Jordan's and Diana's friendship points to the harm that may follow a narrow, restrictive understanding of the place of intimate friendship in the lives of celibates:

> One does meet priests and religious who are obviously good, and indeed holy, but who are in a curious way remote, aloof, "detached"; they will gladly expend their last energies on their official duties, they will do anything to help "souls," they will surely have a very bright crown in heaven; if you wanted an expert answer to some technical question about prayer or piety you would go to them unhesitatingly— but if you were struggling desperately with some purely human, personal problem you would never dream of approaching them. It means surely that though they are holy they are not saints; they are not, humanly speaking, examples of perfect holiness; and they are not saints precisely because there is something *human* lacking to them, their hearts are not fully alive, they have not yet fully realized in themselves the ideal given us under the symbol of the sacred heart of Christ, his *human* love of men [sic].[8]

To the objection that such openness to deep human friendship is particularly dangerous for celibate priests and sisters, Vann answers that Christ did not come so that we might have safety and have it in abundance. He came that we might have life and have it to the full.[9]

[8]Ibid., 52.
[9]Ibid., 51.

"Some of us would indeed give anything to feel safe, about our life in this world as in the next, but we cannot have it both ways: safety or life, we must choose."[10] In the long run, of course, choosing life, choosing to be fully human, is the safest and surest way to a full life in Christ.[11]

In part two of *To Heaven with Diana!*, Vann reprints fifty of Jordan's letters to Diana covering a fourteen-year period from Advent of 1222 to 1236. Jordan's relationship with Diana, especially in the first years of their friendship, reflected a paternal tone of care and protection. Though he continued to greet her as "his beloved daughter in Christ" throughout their correspondence, as the friendship matures and deepens, the two Dominicans see their affection unfold into the parity that is at the heart of all true friendship, regardless of ecclesial or social differences in status. Over the years they became soul-mates in Christ, led by God's grace to mutual interdependence as founding members of the Dominican family. Each burdened with the responsibilities of leadership, their intimate friendship provided support and consolation as they addressed the challenges facing the early years of the Dominican Order.

Three excerpts of Jordan's letters reveal the depth and passion of their love:

> Since it is not given to me, my beloved, to see you with my bodily eyes as often as you would wish and I would wish, nor to find comfort in your presence, my heart finds some slight solace, and a tempering of its longing, when I can visit you by letter and tell you how things are with me. . . .[12]

In a letter written two years later, Jordan writes:

> I cannot find the time to write you the long letter your love would wish for and I would so gladly send; none the less I do write, I send you a very little word, the Word made little in the crib, the Word who was made flesh for us, the Word of salvation and grace, Jesus Christ. . . . Read over this Word in your heart, turn it over in your mind, let it be sweet as honey on your lips; ponder it, dwell on it, that it may dwell with you and in you for ever. There is another word that I send you, small and brief: my love, which will speak for me to your love in your

[10]Ibid., 51–52.

[11]Ibid., 53. Vann observes that "if they [priests] keep their hearts alive and young in them they may fall into fresh follies; if they kill their hearts they will never reach the full glory of their vocation and may well fall into worse disasters, into a living death."

[12]Letter 24, Christmastide, 1227.

heart and will content it. May this word too be yours, and likewise dwell with you for ever.[13]

While it is clear that Diana and Jordan found joy and deep pleasure in their friendship, they also experienced the pain of prolonged separation. Jordan writes:

> The longer we are separated from one another, the greater becomes our desire to see one another again. Yet it is only by God's will (as I hope) that so far I have been prevented from coming to you; and if this was his will, it is for us to bend ours to conformity with it.[14]

This last excerpt underscores a critical and essential element in authentic celibate friendship, especially the friendship between priests and women religious. The needs of the diocese and religious congregation, that is, the assignment to ministry by bishop and religious superior, must come before any considerations of proximity by the celibate friends. The poverty of soul implicit in celibate friendship— no claim can be made on the celibate friend—and the obedience essential to ecclesial ministry will necessarily demand long periods of separation. Should a priest negotiate a ministerial assignment with proximity to a beloved friend in mind, the appropriateness of the friendship may be questioned. Jordan of Saxony and Diana D'Andalo, as Vann's work shows, were blessed with a passionate, intimate friendship. Their remarkable friendship bears a timeless witness to the power of celibate love.

Thomas Merton and M.

Seven centuries later America's most celebrated spiritual writer recorded in his journal the agony and ecstasy of a surprising, intimate relationship with a young nurse, some thirty years his junior. Thomas Merton's love for M., a student nurse who treated him following back surgery in March 1966, and her love for him illustrates the power and force of the heart's desire for union and intimacy. Their problematic friendship and love lead them to ecstatic moments of intimacy and transcendence. Both proclaimed a transformation of soul and heart that left no doubt, at least in their own minds, about the authenticity of their love. The intoxicating joy as well as the anguish, vulnerability, and jealousy of this "odd couple" may simply be too atypical, even too

[13]Letter 31, Christmastide, 1229.
[14]Letter 48, Paris, February–March 1235.

bizarre, to be much help to us in searching for models of celibate relationships of intimacy.

Two factors, however, suggest their relationship deserves attention. First, the range of bliss and conflict of soul experienced by both reveals a crisis of identity and integrity in the celibate lovers. Merton the monk and M. (no further identification appears in the journal), the engaged student nurse, discover complexities, uncertainties, and problems of conscience that shake the foundations of their identities. Both understand that the very earthiness and urgency of their months of correspondence, phone calls, and arranged visits, from March through the summer of 1966, seriously threaten their integrity. Second, Merton, like Jordan of Saxony, provides us with a written record of the friendship. Unlike the passionate calm of Jordan's letters which capture the stability of his friendship with Diana, Merton's entries reflect the profound ambiguity of his volcanic, short-lived relationship with M. The Dominican writes of the sublime element in celibate friendship, the Trappist of his tortured ambivalence. Jordan's letters point to the ideal, Merton's journal entries to the real, down to earth complexity and messiness that can befall intimate, celibate friendship.

Merton's abiding belief in the fundamental rightness of his relationship with M. surfaces in the journal entry of August 6, 1966:

> How beautiful were the few times we had together. I do not regret at all my love for her and am convinced it was a true gift from God and has been an inestimable help to me. I know it was getting to a point where it could have gone very wrong and become destructive. But it did not, and I know it remains in both our lives as something healthy and beautiful, a real grace, that will hold us together forever. I am so thankful for this![15]

Earlier entries, however, reflect considerable self-doubt and vacillation: "It is true I do sincerely love her and I know she loves me too, and we do owe each other something—but all in all it is simply a game, a fascinating, pleasurable exciting game. . . ." (May 16, 1966). The very next day, however, he writes:

> The trouble is that with M. and me it is not a game. What I wrote yesterday was in large part a shameful evasion, since somehow on Sunday I had suddenly convinced myself I had to find a way out—and there is no easy way out of love. The suffering is great but there is no getting around it. . . . It is not a game. That was a wicked thing for me to say. . . . (May 17, 1966).

[15]*Learning to Love: The Journals of Thomas Merton*, vol. 6, 1966–67, ed. Christine M. Bochen (New York: Harper Collins, 1997) 110.

The anguish Merton records is situated to a large extent in the most notable difference between Jordan and Diana and Merton and M.'s relationships. Jordan and Diana are committed celibates. While Merton is a committed celibate, M. certainly is not. She understands that her love for Merton is radically constrained by his monastic vows. Her rational acceptance of the celibate parameters of their love are not easily translated into the longings of her heart. Merton scholar William Shannon believes that the relationship with M. was fundamentally a good experience for him. In M., Merton found a friend who loved him as a man, fully and completely, and not simply as the famous monk and writer. He found he was able to love her with a completeness and ardor that took his breath away. Whether the relationship was ultimately a graced experience for M. remains another question. Only she can answer that and she has chosen to maintain her privacy.[16] While the gift of celibate intimacy resists strict typologies, it settles upon individuals in such a manner that they are left in a state of wonder and thanksgiving.

Writing after his relationship with M. was terminated, Merton observes: "There is a certain fullness in my life now, even without her. Something that was never there before" (September 2, 1966). While wonder and thanksgiving remain the fundamental attitudes of celibate friends, their hearts also experience the pain of sacrifice and separation. "I love her deeply and I can see that the purity of this love does really demand the sacrifice of human comfort and consolation" (August 22, 1966). Then, a little over a week later, Merton writes: "But one thing is sure where love is serious, there is real suffering" (September 2, 1966).

Meeting the soul's essential longing for union and intimacy will from time to time be dangerous. Greater danger awaits, however, for priests and laity alike who willfully determine to live their lives in the pseudo safety of emotional isolation. Still, from Jordan's letters to Diana and Merton's journal entries detailing his relationship with M., it appears that the healthiest—and safest—celibate relationships occur between committed, mature adults. Jordan and Diana experienced the blessing of their relationship as committed celibates bound by and rooted in the Dominican charism. Their intimate friendship was supported and sustained by their common vocations to the Order of Preachers.

Merton and M., on the other hand, experienced the wrenching tension of their radically different life-styles and commitments—the

[16]See William H. Shannon's *Something of a Rebel: Thomas Merton—His Life and Works* (Cincinnati: St. Anthony Messenger Press, 1997) 40–41.

monk in his early fifties, the student nurse in her early twenties; the vowed celibate and the young woman ready for marriage; the solitary and the college co-ed; the spiritual master and the professional novice. These staggering differences in history and temperament cast their passionate love into the shadows of profound ambiguity and anxiety. Yet, in spite of the difficulties, mistakes, and absurdities recorded in Merton's journal, he believed in the ultimate grace and goodness of his intimate friendship with M. True celibate friendship, then, in meeting the divinely created human need for intimacy, strengthens the priest in his commitment to the Gospel and to the responsibilities of his ministry. Merton captures the power and mystery of his truth as a priest and monk in his journal entry of November 16, 1966: "Somehow in the depths of my being I know that love for her [M.] can coexist with my solitude, but everything depends on my fidelity to a vocation that there is no use trying too much to rationalize. It is *there*. It is a root fact of my existence." There remains another dimension to celibate friendship that deserves our attention—that of intimacy and the issue of orientation.

Intimacy and Orientation

The issue of homosexuality and the priesthood is addressed in Chapter 7. Here I want to propose that, from a public, social perspective, celibate, intimate friendship is generally more easily achieved for gay priests than it is for straight priests.[17] Whatever one's sexual orientation might be, celibate friendship holds a certain danger. It is possible that the friendship, especially when there is an erotic dimen-

---

[17]John Boswell comments on the use of "gay" rather than homosexual,

> . . . [I]t seems likely that the scholarly disinclination to employ the word "gay" is due less to enthusiasm about "homosexual" than to a general reluctance on the part of academics to employ popular neologisms. However justifiable this tendency may be generally it is somewhat misguided in this particular case. The word "homosexual," despite its air of antiquity, was actually coined in the late nineteenth century by German psychologists, introduced into English only at the beginning of the present century, and vehemently opposed for decades after its appearance because of its bastard origin and vague connotations. In contrast, "gay" (in the sense under discussion) probably antedates "homosexual" by several centuries and has generally been employed with far greater precision: most speakers use "gay" to describe persons who are conscious of erotic preference for their own gender.

Christianity, Social Tolerance, and Homosexuality (Chicago: The University of Chicago Press, 1980) 42–43.

sion present, will distract the parties from their Gospel-centered, consecrated life-style as well as to their responsibilities to ministry. Both gay and straight priests face similar demands in meeting their need for intimate friendships: fidelity to prayer, unwavering commitment to ministry, and a readiness to discuss the celibate friendship with a spiritual mentor.

While some clergy and laity will fail to understand a celibate's need for close friendships, the healthiest of these relationships will have a certain public character to them. The priest's family and close friends will generally be aware of the friendship and in many cases so will his colleagues in ministry. Although the interpersonal dynamics of straight and gay celibate friendships may have a certain similarity, the social dynamics do not. Precisely because celibate friendship is easily misunderstood, it is generally easier for a gay priest to experience a public, social dimension in a friendship with a man, a dimension that tends to validate and confirm the celibate relationship, than it is for a straight priest in a celibate relationship with a woman. In other words, a priest attending a movie or play with another male is considered socially acceptable; however, it is often problematic for a priest to do so with a female companion.

One of the untold stories of the priesthood at the close of the twentieth century is the large number of life-giving, joyful, loving friendships between celibate priests and their committed friends. Both straight and gay priests have sustained celibate relationships of real grace and depth. From time to time mistakes have been made   some proving to be tragic. And from time to time the struggle to keep a friendship celibate may be intense. Only prudence, honesty, and above all, God's grace can nurture celibate friends into true soul-mates. Like Jordan of Saxony and Thomas Merton, priests gifted with authentic celibate relationships often discover a transformation of soul, a compassion and strength previously unknown to them. In spite of the confusion and ambiguity that sooner or later surfaces, in spite of the suffering that inevitably touches all human love and friendship, priests blessed with celibate, loving intimacy give thanks for the wonder of it all. In the process, they believe they have grown as men of God, as men of the Church.

Part II
Challenges

4

Facing the Unconscious

Laius, king of Thebes, is told by an oracle
that he will be killed by his son.
When a baby is born to his wife, Jocasta,
Laius orders Oedipus killed, but a shepherd rescues him.
When Oedipus becomes a young man, he learns from an oracle
that he will kill his father and marry his mother.
Troubled by this news, Oedipus flees,
and on a journey he quarrels with a man and kills him,
not knowing he is Laius, his true father.
Oedipus is then posed a riddle, which he solves;
he is made king of Thebes and marries the widowed Queen Jocasta,
unaware that she is his mother.

—The Oedipus myth

To accept oneself as one is may sound like a simple thing,
but simple things are always the most difficult things to do.
In actual life to be simple and straightforward is an art in itself
requiring the greatest discipline,
while the question of self-acceptance
lies at the root of the moral problem
and at the heart of a whole philosophy of life.

—C. G. Jung

In spite of the unprecedented challenges and ordeals engulfing the priesthood at the turn of the millennium, the *esprit d'corps* long associated with Catholic clergy refuses to buckle. The fraternity holds. As the millennium's first rays of dawn catch the contours of the changing face of the priesthood, priests still sense they are members of a mysterious brotherhood that continues to shape their lives and world-view. Not only is their pastoral identity grounded in the covenant of ordination, they experience a spiritual bond linking them to priests the world over, indeed to priests from ages past and to the priests of ages yet to come.

At the same time the polarization of the last decades of the twentieth century and the first decades of the twenty-first has left its own mark on priests as well as the Church at large. As a result there is more caution and reticence discernible when priests meet for the first time. Priests who have known each other for decades, while sensing the differing theologies and pastoral visions that have created tension and in some cases mistrust in their relationships, still sense a commonality that transcends the unsettling differences. For the same priestly archetype has marked each of them. Their spiritual journey as well as their ministry as presbyters bond them on a deep and inexplicable level unique to their fraternity, especially when, as in the Latin rite, priesthood is linked to celibacy. They have chosen to walk the same path of discipleship and along the way have come to understand that they share many of the same crosses and joys, the same pain, and the same privilege. Years of pastoral ministry have burnt off the innocent idealism of their early years. Few are naïve. Few priests labor under illusions. They know the human condition better than any bartender or taxi driver. Their work as priests provides access to the inner chambers of their parishioners' souls and there, seated quietly, as trusted guests, they witness betrayal and infidelity, forgiveness and understanding, mercy and reconciliation. Such access and intimacy to the marking moments of people's lives give a certain quality of soul to priests. It's as if they share the same ecclesial genes—the same tribal blood running through their veins.

Priests who meet regularly for prayer, conversation, and a meal epitomize this fraternity. The *Jesus Caritas* and *Emmaus* programs, and similar support groups for priests, have reminded them of their need for close, trusting relationships with their brothers in ministry. Among themselves they relax into the truth that they are brothers in Christ. Catholics as well as others who have come to know priests well are fascinated and intrigued by this unofficial, worldwide fraternity. Even priests who claim to like priests but can't stand gatherings of clergy acknowledge that there is a mysterious communion linking them with other priests that goes beyond the insights and analysis of sociologists and social theorists.

From a social science point of view, the priesthood is arguably the most significant subgroup the Church has known. This sacramental, ritualized brotherhood, however, has its own shadow side. Whenever psychic energy is profoundly crystallized and mobilized as it is in the rite of ordination into the celibate priesthood, the depth dimension deserves attention. Failure to attend to the unconscious or pre-conscious aspects of the priestly fraternity results in real danger for the priest. His identity, integrity, and capacity for deep personal relating are threatened. The consequent spiritual upheaval is baffling to the priest and his spiritual director and confidants. Many, I believe, have interpreted this inner suffering to be a sign that priesthood is really not their calling, not their truth.

Operating just below the surface of consciousness, a complex of psychic forces encourage behaviors and attitudes which subvert his conscious desire to serve the people of God. Included among these attitudes and behaviors are clericalism, elitism, careerism, legalism, envy, and competition. When gripped by these psychic forces it is easy for the priest to over-identify with his priestly persona and thereby lose touch with his baptismal identity. The need to buffet his exalted priestly identity may well abort his potential for honest relationships with men and women. His priestly persona becomes his rock of identity and the wellspring of his solace. The subtle balance between his baptismal and priestly identities is lost. The line is crossed and he treasures the bitter-sweet belief that *he is not like other men*. What explains these elitist attitudes, the barely disguised envy and jealousy of brother priests, and the surprising passivity common to many priests? What will we find if we take an unblinking look into the unconscious dynamics which shape and influence the lives and inner worlds of priests?

A New Look at an Old Myth

It is more than sixty years now since Sigmund Freud's death. Clergy continue to be wary of this pioneer of the unconscious and for good reason. His anthropology appears seriously flawed in the light of contemporary philosophical and psychoanalytic theory. The rejection of any teleology, any transcendent purpose and meaning to life, places Freud's psychoanalytic theory in radical conflict with the faith perspective of the world's major religions of the book. At the same time, a too quick dismissal of Freud's remarkable blueprint of the unconscious and his discovery of the subterranean dynamics of the human psyche would be unfortunate.[1] I propose here that a fresh look at

[1]Hans Küng, "Religion: The Final Taboo?" *Origins,* vol. 16, no. 1 (May 22, 1986).

There can be no "return to a pre-Freudian state" since the discovery of the influence exerted by psychodynamic unconscious factors and particularly by

Freud's famous Oedipal complex reveals a psychic drama that sheds a compassionate light on the hidden pitfalls the priest must navigate on his journey to maturity and psychic wholeness.[2]

We can identify at least three major "readings" of the now famous Oedipal complex—the mechanistic, the dynamic, and the iconic, each with numerous sub-readings.[3] Our point of departure is inspired by the third of these, the iconic or metaphorical reading. Rather than focusing on the traditional and literal interpretations of the complex—the young boy so desirous of possessing his mother that he wishes to dispose of his father—the metaphorical readings present us with meanings that transcend the libidinous character of the mechanistic reading while recognizing the foundational role of the Oedipal project in human development.[4]

Approaching the Oedipal complex from the expanded horizon of metaphor while respecting the dynamic family tension inherent to the primal Oedipal theory sheds considerable light on the unspoken, unnamed tensions bubbling below the surface in the life of the priest. Oedipus, in this light, desires to be his mother's only love. Awakening to the special adult-to-adult intimacy his mother and father share shakes the foundations of his psychic security. Oedipus wants his

---

the earliest parent child relationship (and thus of sexuality in the broadest sense of the word) on religion, more precisely on the image of God and on the distinction between good and evil. Religion since that discovery, must also submit to psychological analysis (28).

[2]Bruno Bettelheim, *The Uses of Enchantment* (New York: Vantage, 1977).

. . . (The) famous myth of Oedipus, through psychoanalytic writings, has become the metaphor by which we refer to a particular emotional constellation within the family—one that can cause the most severe impediments to growing up into a mature well-integrated person, while being, on the other hand, the potential source of the richest personality development (195).

[3]For a summary of these readings, see Peter Homans, *Theology after Freud* (New York: The Bobbs-Merrill Company, 1970) 3–14, and chapter 5 which reviews the iconic Oedipal interpretations of Norman O. Brown, David Bakan, and Philip Rieff, 117–59.

[4]It is difficult to exaggerate the significance of Ernest Becker's *Denial of Death* (New York: The Free Press, 1973) as an iconic interpretation of Freud's Oedipal theory. See also, Paul Ricoeur, *Freud and Philosophy: An Essay on Interpretation,* trans. Denis Savage (New Haven: Yale University Press, 1970).

Every reader of Freud's early Writings is struck by the decisive manner in which the Oedipus complex was discovered; in one stroke it was revealed both as an individual drama and as the collective fate of mankind, as a psychological fact and as the source of morality, as the origin of neurosis and as the origin of civilization (188).

mother's attention and love exclusively. She is his first love object and his natural self-absorption simply cannot tolerate less than her total and exclusive love. Rather than the desire to kill his father and marry his mother, the son desires to be her only love. He is jealous not only of his father but of his siblings who also bask in the love of his mother. Oedipus' self-definition and his sense of personal meaning are grounded in his experience of being his mother's one and only love.

In this light, father, brother, and sister are all competitors. The undisturbed bliss of being alone the object of his mother's love has been irrevocably shattered by the realization that she belongs to others as well as to him. Unable to fathom the dignity of his place in the family circle, that his mother is able to love others without diminishing her love for him, Oedipus is filled with jealousy and rage. Impotent in face of the father's infinitely superior position and his parents' unconditional acceptance of his siblings, the boy Oedipus resolves his Oedipal conflict by surrendering his outlandish claim to the exclusive love of his mother by identifying with his father. He accepts his authority and concedes that he is not the only son. He is loved, but loved as one son with siblings who are equally loved. The repression of his desire for the exclusive affection of his mother has tamed his polymorphous libidinous desire. He has negotiated the politics of the family. Reason has triumphed over instinct.

The anxiety at the center of Oedipal conflict has been relieved, at least temporarily, as the young boy gets on with his life. Underneath the veneer of his social adaptation, however, lurks residual forces of the Oedipal complex. He remains prone to maneuvering for the favorite son position in the family's social ordering. He finds he is disposed to jealousy and envy at the accomplishments of his brothers and sisters. Now that his socialization and domestication are so thoroughly accomplished, he is unaware of his unconscious residual desire to return to his symbiotic, all satisfying, exclusive relationship with his mother.

From the metaphoric or iconic perspective, Oedipal tension is about being first, being "number one," at least from a psychological perspective. On the conscious level the young boy not only understands but delights in the special love of his mother and father. He welcomes the companionship of his brothers and sisters. On the surface, all appears as it should be. The brothers and sisters fight from time to time or even most of the time. Seldom, however, is there overt evidence of deep-seated hatred or destructive envy. Yet the sibling rivalry that is almost universally recognized as inherent to family life points to residual Oedipal tension that often endures well beyond the early years of childhood.

From a developmental perspective, the *complex* of the Oedipal drama tends to hibernate in the inner caves of the unconscious until awakened by conflicts that mirror the original, primal scene. The painful efforts to find one's place in the in-between-years of adolescence, the wrenching, jealous agony of failed love, the small-mindedness characteristic of siblings at the reading of their parents' wills, the ruthless climbing of the corporate and social ladders, barely concealed resentment at the success and achievements of colleagues and peers, all point to a stirring of the Oedipal dynamic. The excessive, often-ruthless competition so blatant in sports and commerce and the irrational, bloody ethnic fighting insidious to Western civilization likewise reveal entrenched Oedipal conflict on the social and national levels.

This Oedipal desire to be the center of the world, to be loved and admired as no one else, to be first among one's siblings and peers, to possess all power and knowledge, to be *special*, is from the psychoanalytic perspective, *the* original sin.[5] Oedipal envy, whose roots are buried deep in the sludge of Oedipal pride, proposes a psychoanalytic equivalent to the Christian doctrine of original sin. In this scenario, the innocent, self-satisfying bliss of pre-Oedipal existence is rudely shattered as the Oedipal drama awakens ego-awareness. A new reality must be faced. "I am not the center of it all, after all. I am *not* God. I am not omnipotent. I am vulnerable, dependent. Most terrible of all, I sense I am subject to annihilation."[6] The iconic reading of

[5]See Paul C. Vitz and John Gartner, "Christianity and Psychoanalysis, Part I: Jesus as the Anti-Oedipus," *Journal of Psychology and Theology*, vol. 12, no. 1 (1984) 4–14. Vitz and Gartner argue that Oedipal motivation is a reasonably apt characterization of original sin.

[6]See Ernest Becker, *The Denial of Death* (New York: The Free Press, 1973). See also Silvano Arieti, *Creativity: The Magic Synthesis* (New York: Basic Books, 1976).

    . . . Oedipus Rex can be said to portray the relation between good and evil, or between truth and illusion (or knowledge and ignorance). Oedipus does not know that he is the killer of his father and the husband of his own mother. The whole drama is a series of events that lead to the discovery of the truth. When he knows the truth, Oedipus feels he has to pay the penalty for his horrendous actions; he gives up the throne and blinds himself. . . . The play portrays the limitation of human consciousness rather than Oedipus' incestuous desire for his mother. His "crime" was actually that of not knowing or not "seeing." He had not been perceptive enough of the many clues, some subliminal, that were in his surroundings. He certainly would not have done what he did, had he known; but the idea of using his ignorance as an alibi did not occur to him. The limitation of his consciousness did not limit the severity of his conscience. Or could it be that Freud, in addition to the idea of the

Oedipus calls to mind the *bad faith* that is so destructive to the priest's integrity. It is an illusion for priests to believe that they can minister well as priests and speak God's prophetic word without "seeing" what is before their eyes and honestly facing it.

The subsequent intolerable anxiety suggests a resolution. A less than total surrender is made in which the young boy accepts his place, identifies with his father, and concedes that his siblings are equally the recipients of his parents' love. As we have seen, the anxiety is assuaged; the process of socialization begins. A certain residue of Oedipal conflict, however, has left its mark on the walls of the psychic underworld. Like the fatal flaw of original sin, this Oedipal residue surfaces in malevolent and multivalent ways, undermining friendships and marriages, conflicting interactions with authority, sowing seeds of jealousy and resentment. This metaphoric reading of the classic Oedipal drama reveals the primary human ordeal. Failure to negotiate the conflict augers poorly for the young boy's future. At the core of the unconscious, therefore, we discover the fundamental human wound: arrogant, demanding subjectivity, whose incessant festering—insidious envy—continues to spawn violence, war, and unthinkable acts of human cruelty. On the communal, interpersonal level, the Oedipal wound betrays our promises of love and fidelity.

Unresolved Oedipal conflict, viewed from this reading of the iconic cluster of Oedipal interpretations, suggests a tenable hermeneutic as we labor to understand the rage and envy, the terrorism and intolerance, characteristic of the *fin-de-siècle* and the first years of the twenty-first century. In the ordinary rhythm of ordinary lives it offers some understanding of the irrational attitudes and behaviors that sabotage so many well-intentioned endeavors. In the lives of priests, we shall see, Oedipal conflict provides at least a glimmer of insight into the tension and conflict common to their relationships with their bishops and brother priests.

Before turning to the role Oedipal conflict plays in the lives of priests, it deserves to be put in its place. Even the third major reading of Freud, what we have called the iconic reading, which has creatively

---

Oedipus complex, found in this tragedy the inspiration for his concepts of the unconscious and of repression? That is, one could also conjecture that perhaps Oedipus did not see because he did not *want* to see.

Oedipus' self-inflicted punishment is also a concretization which becomes symbolic: he blinds himself. Since he would not "see" in a more abstract way, he feels he does not deserve to see. . . . The only person who really "saw" and knew was the blind prophet, Tiresias (151–52).

been fleshed out by thinkers of the stature of Paul Ricoeur, Norman O. Brown, and Philip Rieff, while proving to be a mother-load of anthropological knowledge, is mined only with considerable risk. One of the more serious dangers found even in an iconic reading of Freud was captured over a quarter century ago by theologian Gregory Baum:

> Freud's theory . . . reflects the middle class environment characteristic of European society at the turn of the century. Freud did not realize that by making Oedipus Rex the normative myth of human life, he excluded women from his essential imagination; the typical human being was male. While I have no doubt that to this day, for vast numbers of people in Western culture, the Oedipal story is still a central model of self-knowledge and personal deliverance, nevertheless by investing this story with universal validity, orthodox Freudian psychoanalysis becomes an ideology that subjects people to a preconceived image and possibly imprisons them in a false imagination.[7]

The Presbyteral Oedipal Complex

Drawing on the iconic reading of the great myth of Oedipus, I have come to see that ordination into the ministerial priesthood, especially in the celibate, Latin rite of the Catholic Church, constellates a fresh Oedipal configuration, a "presbyteral Oedipal complex." Here the Oedipal triangle reveals the newly ordained priest as the son, the diocesan bishop as the father, and the Church, of course, the mother. It is not unusual to hear an ordaining bishop turn to the parents of the men just ordained to thank them for the gift of their sons to the Church. They are encouraged by the bishop to trust in the Church's care and solicitude for their sons now ordained priests. The Church will love them as a mother loves her children, the bishop will look after them as a father looks after his sons. Often the parents are reminded that their sons have joined a unique brotherhood in which they will find men of like mind and heart, men who will be like brothers to them.

The other side of the sacramental character of ordination, then, is the psychic birthing of the newly ordained priest, in a profound archetypal covenant, with the Church, his bishop, and his brother priests. The sacred power and psychic force of this covenant commitment to bishop-father, Church-mother, and priest-brothers and they to him has been dramatized in film and theater, in folklore and literature. Its mysterious reality fascinates the imagination of Catholics as well as those with little understanding of the Catholic imagination. Often, it appears, the priest naïvely enters into the fellowship of his new sacra-

[7]Gregory Baum, *Religion and Alienation* (New York: Paulist Press, 1975) 122.

mental family with little understanding of the struggles and conflicts that await him. Family life after Freud, we now know, is far more complex than previously understood. All the psychic forces we know to be at work in the family of origin—unconscious jockeying to be the parents' favorite, sibling rivalry, willful ambition—all these negative dynamics are now in place and ready to erupt in the life of the newly ordained priest.

The first years after ordination are relatively free of Oedipal conflict. The newly ordained priest is buoyed up by the clear and unequivocal affirmation of his bishop. His parishioners make real the affection and approval of the mother-Church and the newness of it all, the wonder and excitement of preaching and presiding at Eucharist, of teaching and counseling, leave little room for competition to surface with his classmates and brother priests. He enjoys a kind of pre-Oedipal bliss which, sadly, is short-lived. The first stirrings of Oedipal conflict often occur when a priest-classmate is chosen for post-seminary graduate studies or is named to an important diocesan post or asked to assume a pastorate. Or the priest simply begins to compare his first assignment with the assignments of his classmates. Why is it that these others were appointed to more attractive parishes? As he hears of the successes of his classmates and brother priests, he notices a twinge of envy.

An example may be helpful here. Years ago while I was teaching at a Catholic liberal arts college for women, I served as the spiritual director for a priest who was a nationally recognized scholar in his field. His books were definitive in his field of study, he lectured widely, and was a beloved professor to his students. He was a genuinely holy and humble man whom I came to admire deeply. At one of our meetings, he began by saying that he had read a few days before an op/ed piece I had written for the local newspaper. He liked it quite a bit. But he then said that as soon as he saw the by-line, he felt a strong twinge of envy or jealousy. Here was a noted scholar, a full professor, a popular lecturer, confessing to emotions that completely baffled him. Our common priestly brotherhood offered some understanding of his envy.

It is not uncommon for newly ordained priests to join presbyterates that number hundreds of priests. Sooner or later, the sheer number of their brother priests undercuts the illusion of their special, unique place in the eyes of their bishop and under the weight of the routine following upon the exhilarating first years of priesthood, many of these men begin to feel that they are simply filling a slot on the personnel charts mounted on chancery office walls. The personal bond experienced at the time of his ordination with his bishop begins to wane. Consciously he understands that he is one of many and the bishop must relate to scores of priests. Still, irrationally, he seeks the special approval of his bishop-father. He waits for some signal that he is thought well of by this father-figure. He waits and observes, carefully calculating the attention given to other priests, mentally marking their assignments and achievements. He notes who is in and who is out in official diocesan circles. By the time of his second assignment, the maternal affection he sensed from the universal Church also wanes.

This maternal Church, while supportive and pointing to his dignity as a priest, is also demanding and controlling. His sexuality is restrained, his dress is determined, his residence assigned. This mother wants him for herself. The defining decisions most men make as they claim their personal ground as men are denied. At the same time, the ecclesial mother in partnership with his father-bishop provides identity, status, and security. Add to this the rich and meaningful life of pastoral leadership and service and you have the makings of a well-established Oedipal conflict. The strong undercurrents of anxiety and restlessness easily go unnamed and if they remain unnamed, as a matter of course, lead to a simmering envy and rage that for the most part remain just below the boiling point. Add to this mostly hidden psychic drama the inevitable stress of pastoral ministry in a Church wrestling with its post-conciliar, renewed understanding of its identity and mission and you have an environment that will tax the healthiest of priests. Relief is sought often in destructive patterns of behavior to both priest and parishioner.

Resolving the Presbyteral Oedipal Complex

Our iconic reading of Freud's Oedipal drama as reconstellated in the unconscious of the newly ordained proposes a kind of template unmasking the psychic challenges and ordeals that sooner or later befall the priest. The naming of these challenges and ordeals remains important and sometimes crucial to the priest's spiritual and personal well-being. Non-negotiated Oedipal conflict leaves the priest prone to nagging doubts concerning the issues of identity and integrity as well as his capacity for authentic, life-giving relationships. Aware of chronic inner disquietude, and unable to name its origin, he intensifies his prayer life, makes plans for another retreat, considers a new spiritual director, ponders the possibility of counseling. Even when these decisions are sustained and fulfilled, the discomfort often shows no sign of diminishment. Recognizing and accepting the unconscious conflict that is disturbing his soul allows grace and healing to anoint his psychic wound and transform his troubled spirit.

Ultimately, of course, it is grace that heals all wounds—psychic, moral, and emotional. Salvation is the balm of the Spirit anointing again and again the broken human spirit. The Oedipus wound, both the family of origin drama and the ecclesial or presbyteral drama are grounded in the primal wound that we call original sin. What happens, then, when these archetypal wounds receive the attention they deserve?

There is a place, perhaps known only to hero-priests, where their courage is tested, where their faith matures. In this place they become men, or find their manhood confirmed. In this place of the soul, they live out the ancient Greek myth of Oedipus. Whenever they face and conquer this ordeal, always the primary work of grace, they both find their own salvation and further the reign of the Gospel. Where they fail to resolve their presbyteral Oedipal complex, they suffer loss of soul and their priesthood becomes effete. The psychic, unannounced task of every priest who has moved through the first, pre-Oedipal years of priesthood into the grip of his presbyteral Oedipal complex, is to find the courage to endure a subtle but enduring tension—to stand in the fire of purification as a man of God committed to servant leadership as a tender of the Word. The tension follows upon his covenant commitment to be both a man of the Church and, at the same time, his own person.

Just as the young boy resolves his primary Oedipal complex by finding the moral courage to be a committed member of his family, quietly facing the undercurrent of forces surfacing as envy and competition, while establishing his own identity as an individual distinct from his family, so the priest must suffer the anxiety and tension of being loyal to the Church and faithful to his own vision. To bear this tension is to stand in a purifying fire that transforms the priest into a liberated man of the Gospel. Such a priest becomes an icon of Christ, a sacramental blessing to any community to which he is called.

The moral courage to effect this passage from psychic immaturity to full maturity in Christ is staggering. From every side he is cajoled to simply stop thinking and buy, uncritically, into the system. Should he succumb to this temptation he is likely to be rewarded. His own inner anxiety appears to recede and his ecclesiastical superiors take note of his docility and deference. Often advancement in a career track is remarkably swift. The rewards of the clerical system quell the doubts of his soul. Finally he surrenders to the artificiality of the clerical world. This world both sustains him and defines him. Whatever the cost, he must enjoy the approval of his father-bishop and maintain the symbiotic union with his mother-Church. Only in this manner can he assuage the anxiety and restlessness of his soul. Only in this manner can he quiet the unruly urges of his sexuality with the erotic fulfillment of clerical power and status. He is blinded to a fatal transformation—he has been taken over by his priestly persona. He no longer is a man like other human beings, a Christian like other Christians. He no longer is one of the faithful. His priestly identity overshadows his baptismal identity. He is Oedipus, aligned with his father-bishop, the special beloved son of his mother-Church. The desire to be like his father—to be a bishop—is carefully hidden. His blind, unthinking loyalty to his mother-Church is worn as a badge of honor.

Competition with his siblings is, for the most part, over. What brother or sister, save a blood brother priest, can compete? If the priest's bishop has not dealt with his own Oedipal conflict, he will unwittingly, and perhaps consciously, sustain and even foster unhealthy Oedipal allegiance in the ranks of the presbyterate. A cadre of "yes men" soothes the Oedipal tensions built into any presbyterate, giving the diocesan bishop a false sense of harmony and fraternity.

A man of the Church. As a man of the Church, he knows what really matters, what it means to be a member of the Church called to servant-leadership. He is blessed with a deep and abiding sense of the Spirit's presence, directing, sustaining, and renewing the Church. His love for the Church does not blind him to the Church's sinfulness. But the Church's sinfulness does not overshadow her mysterious power to transform the world, to be *the* key player in the unfolding of the reign of God. He knows his church history and is not scandalized. He is proud of his humbling call to priestly ministry, but more proud of his baptismal call to discipleship and holiness. He possesses the courage to stand in loyal opposition should official church policy appear unfaithful to the Gospel of Christ. He draws courage from those "friends of God and prophets" with whom he makes up the communion of saints.[8] He works readily with lay and religious pastoral ministers. He rejoices in their talents and pastoral skills, trusting that God's spirit is loose in the Church and loose in the world.[9]

His own man. Our iconic reading of Freud draws into bold relief two poles which shape the identity and determine the integrity of the priest—the communal and the individual dimensions to his existence. Just as the primary Oedipal conflict requires that a youth identify with his family and at the same time establish his independence and identity as someone united to but distinct from his family of origin, so the

[8]See Elizabeth Johnson's *Friends of God and Prophets* (New York: Continuum, 1998).

[9]See Thomas F. O'Meara's *Loose in the World* (New York: Paulist Press, 1974).

priest must resolve his presbyteral Oedipal conflict by finding the courage to be his own man while simultaneously remaining a man of the Church. While following the wisdom of the ancients in "thinking with the Church," he also is fearless in thinking for himself. His theological reflection on his own pastoral experience and the events of his world, while done in communion with his companions in ministry and his parishioners, transcends "group think." He stands his ground with a quiet and humble courage, open to the gifts and wisdom of his ecclesial superiors and his brothers and sisters in the communion of saints. Faithful to the Church as a man of the Church must be, he is faithful to his own integrity and authenticity, sometimes with great, though hidden, moral heroism. While showing appropriate deference to his bishop and loyalty to his brother priests, they know where he stands. His integrity garners the respect of his friends and parishioners. His authenticity allows him to speak with authority and conviction. Through these twin fidelities the priest becomes a man of the word.

The path through the presbyteral Oedipal complex, unfortunately, is barely discernible. Hints of a trail can be seen here and there, but more often than not it is the direction taken by those who seek security over the exhilarating freedom of the Gospel. The priest-seeker who fearlessly presses on as a man of faith and prayer finds his way. Most priests, I believe, discover this path leading to true spiritual adulthood and come to see that their *truth,* their vocation, is grounded in the ministerial priesthood of Jesus Christ. They are *one* of the bishop's men who rejoice in their special role in the mission of the Church. They are *adult* sons of mother Church who can fend for themselves, who are free of adolescent dependence and insecurity. For these men, to be something other than a priest is an "existential inability."[10]

There are priests, however, that cannot bear to stand in the fire leading to true adulthood. The tension and accompanying ambivalence found in standing both as a man of the Church and their own man is too much. They follow one of two false paths: either becoming sycophant ecclesiastics and pious, effete clerics or the less common but equally destructive path of the maverick. The priest who embraces the latter path feels compelled to reject and attack any initiative his bishop may undertake. The bishop, any bishop, is always the enemy and the institutional Church is never to be trusted. Both paths reveal severe authority problems and suggest that the priests who choose them endured troubled relationships with their birth fathers.

[10]Edward Schillebeeckx, *Celibacy,* trans. C.A.L. Jarrott (New York: Sheed and Ward, 1968).

The resolution of presbyteral Oedipal conflict, of course, is greatly assisted by diocesan bishops who have basically worked through their own family and presbyteral tensions. These episcopal leaders model both ecclesial loyalty and personal integrity. Their fidelity to the Gospel, the college of bishops, and to the pope is manifest. They listen to the people of God and to their priests as true partners in dialogue. Bishops of this cut, by their very integrity and authenticity, inspire their priests to be true men of the Church who reflect on their pastoral experience with both a knowledge of the church's history and tradition while trusting their pastoral vision. They inspire their priests to be men who bravely yet humbly dare to think. Less secure bishops, however, encourage and reward an unthinking docility that cannot help but to strengthen the priest's Oedipal conflict. Eventually the entrenched pattern of dependent relating to the bishop weakens priestly morale and integrity.

Often the fabled priests of a diocese are revered precisely because they were clearly committed churchmen and at the same time men who knew how to hold their ground in dealing both with their bishops and parishioners. At priest gatherings, senior and middle-aged priests regularly regale the more recently ordained with stories of these men that shape the common story of a given presbyterate. Underneath these stories, however, the integrity of these fabled men reflect commitment, courage, and an authenticity that easily captures the imagination of the younger priests. They became the giants of the presbyterate because they managed to be individuals of deep faith and loyalty while refusing to be taken over by their priestly personae. They had, with grit and humor, worked through their priestly Oedipal conflict.

The Episcopal Oedipal Complex

Elevation to the episcopacy, viewed from the lens of the iconic reading of Freud's Oedipal drama, reflects a similar unconscious configuration to that of the newly ordained priest. Only here, the newly ordained bishop assumes the role of the boy Oedipus, the pope that of the father, and the Church, as in the presbyteral Oedipal drama, again manifesting the maternal corner of the triangle. At first there is little if any evidence of Oedipal turbulence. He has been named bishop, after all, by the pope himself. He savors the affirmation of his faithful commitment to the priesthood signified by his selection as bishop. He now is linked in a special way to the universal mother-Church. He responds to her affirming nod with a solemn oath to defend the unity of the

Church and the integrity of the faith. While he takes his place among the college of bishops, a body of brothers who will provide an important safety net to the psychological dangers he will face, the controlling psychic dynamic is that of son to the pope and Church. Though most often in his middle years or beyond, the priest now bishop faces an interior struggle that may threaten his soul's integrity.

The resolution is obvious. By God's grace the bishop is clearly a man of the Church, a shepherd of the Church, an icon of Christ. All this he must be and more. For as a bishop he is anointed to be a kind of martyr for the Church. He is prepared by grace and anointing to bear witness to Jesus Christ and the mission of the Church even to the point of death. At the same time, as a member of the college of bishops, he must speak his truth humbly and with courage to his brother bishops and to the bishop of Rome. As a diocesan bishop, he must find the courage to be faithful to his own lights, to the needs of his local church, and to his reading of a broken, wounded world. Looking back on a century marked by Vatican centralization, standing one's ground as a bishop often requires heroic moral courage. Without looking too hard, sibling rivalry and competition can be observed within the fraternity of bishops. Episcopal Oedipal tension is, after all, essentially the same tension facing the priest. The challenge and resolution are, likewise, essentially the same: to be at the same time a man of the Church and one's own man.

Christ and Oedipus

Like us in all but sin, the fully human Jesus of Nazareth's psyche bore the template of Oedipal conflict. As a boy like other boys he was predisposed for the awakening of the drama that shapes the character and tests the mettle of male children. But Jesus, graced as no other human ever before or ever after, betrays not the slightest inkling of Oedipal envy or jealousy. His divinity did not exempt him from the patterns and stages of human development. Nor did the saintly character of his parents negate all evidence of Oedipal conflict. Although the holiness and grace-filled integrity of the humble Nazareth household defused the potentially destructive aspects of the Oedipal drama, the inevitable human tensions inherent to even the saintliest of households was surely present as we shall see. The boy Jesus lived—and related—in a manner that evidenced only the slightest residue of the Oedipal template and the merest hint of Oedipal conflict.

An observant young Jew, Jesus was well versed in his religious tradition. "After three days they found him in the temple, sitting in the midst of the teachers, listening to them and asking them questions, and all who heard him were astounded at his understanding and his answers."[11] Although his religious knowledge and spiritual wisdom led to amazement in the elders of his day, the compelling power of his person is more often linked to the radical authenticity and integrity that captured the souls and imaginations of those who came into the circle of his influence. No one was more obedient and more free. No one was more spiritual and more real, more of the earth. No one less self-absorbed and more self-possessed. No teacher was less authoritarian and more authoritative.

From this perspective Jesus was his own man as no one has ever been his own man, or her own woman. Nothing could dissuade him from following his destiny as savior of the world, nothing could shackle his freedom as God's beloved son. Jesus' fidelity to his truth as the Word made flesh and his freedom from all envy and jealousy point to the new order, the new being to which he calls each and every human being.[12] The Oedipal dynamics that grip young boys and men at different stages of their development were soothed and calmed by Jesus' unscathed integrity and authenticity. His peace of soul—a peace the world cannot give—served as the clearest signal that Oedipal conflict had been transformed.[13]

The Temple drama at Passover in Luke 2 alluded to above is the earliest evidence the Scriptures provide of Jesus' unwavering commitment to his truth and to the fulfillment of his messianic mission—the essence of Oedipal transformation.

> When his parents saw him, they were astonished, and his mother said to him: "Son, why have you done this to us? Your father and I have been looking for you with great anxiety." And he said to them: "Why were you looking for me? Did you not know that I must be in my Father's house?" But they did not grasp what he said to them. He went down with them then, and came to Nazareth, and was obedient to them. His mother meanwhile kept all these things in memory. Jesus, for his part, progressed in wisdom and age and grace before God and men.[14]

[11]Luke 2:46-47.

[12]2 Cor 5:17 and Gal 6:15.

[13]Sigmund Freud, "A Child Is Being Beaten," *The Standard Edition of the Complete Psychological Works of Sigmund Freud*, vol. 17, ed. and trans. J. Strachey (London: Hogarth Press) 79–204. Freud believed that the Oedipal complex was never truly resolved and could be awakened at key developmental stages such as puberty.

[14]Luke 2:48-52.

We see here an exquisite tension in the conversation between Mary and Jesus. "Son, why have you done this to us?" Jesus responds by declaring that he must be true to his own truth. For Jesus to be his "own man" was to courageously accomplish his mission. Yes, he was a loyal member of his family, but he would not let even the anxiety and worry of his parents deter him from obedience to his father. If fidelity to one's birth family, i.e., being committed to his primary community, his origin of birth family, and for the priest, his ecclesial family, is one pole of the Oedipal dialectic, the other is the integrity to stand outside that community when necessary—to be one's own person.

The great lesson contained in these few verses in Luke is that the priest's fidelity to the Church (being a man of the Church) and the courageous guarding of his own integrity (being his own man) are resolved in his personal commitment to the Word and person of Jesus Christ. In Christ he becomes a true man of the Church and his true self.

Still other New Testament passages capture both Jesus' Oedipal courage to assert his mission and his prophetic independence to be the Word made flesh. On the surface, Jesus appears to be insensitive to his mother and family. In the third chapter of Mark's Gospel we read,

> His mother and his brothers arrived. Standing outside they sent word to him and called him. A crowd seated around him told him, "Your mother and your brothers [and your sisters] are outside asking for you." But he said to them in reply, "Who are my mother and [my] brothers?" And looking around at those seated in the circle he said, "Here are my mother and my brothers. [For] whoever does the will of God is my brother and sister and mother."[15]

At the wedding in Cana, Jesus resolves a moment of ambivalence—his own sense of timing and his desire to honor the request of his mother—by uttering a direct, almost harsh word to her. To Mary's, "They have no more wine," Jesus responds, "Woman, how does your concern affect me? My hour has not yet come."[16] The exchange is critical for it provides a glimpse into the loving yet adult and mature relationship between the two.

Our reading of Freud's epic drama suggests that unresolved maternal Oedipal tension can be observed in mothers who have an inclination or even a compulsion to control the lives of their children. From an institutional perspective, a Church's desire to control her "children," even for the noblest of intentions, suggests an Oedipal dynamic that holds both "mother" and "child" in a truncated, immature

[15]Mark 3:31-35.
[16]John 2:3-4.

relationship. Mary's response to Jesus, taken in this light, is quite remarkable. The text from John gives no hint of either a mother using guilt to persuade a child to comply with her wishes or resentment in the adult child responding to her request. She simply says: "Do whatever he tells you."[17] Behind and beyond this dialogue, a profound reality of mature trust and unspeakable affection is revealed. The mother-son relationship is devoid of both sentimentality and unconscious maneuvering. Mary, it is clear, was incapable of playing the proud but controlling mother; there is not a hint of "my son the messiah!"

Our iconic Oedipal reading provides an arresting hermeneutic for the priest-mother relationship so fundamental to family dynamics that include a priest-son. Often the definitive resolution to Oedipal tension occurs when a young man leaves home to marry. Still a member of his family, he leaves the security of his parents home to become his own man. The celibate priest, however, is not only the unmarried son, but the son committed to remain unmarried, and as such often enjoys a particular emotional bonding with his mother. Especially when his mother is widowed, the son without spouse and children regularly has more time for his mother. His mother understands that her priest-son does not have the emotional fulfillment that spouse and children provide for his married brothers and sisters. Aware of his human neediness and his special dignity as a priest, he becomes her special prize.

Being the "mother of a priest" still conveys considerable social status in Catholic circles. Clearly, the close relationship between mother and her priest-son is understandable and can be quite healthy. Both mother and son, however, need to make their relationship exemplify that of two emotionally mature adults, a relationship that reflects the same absence of sentimentality and unconscious control which characterized the relationship of Jesus and Mary. Should there be considerable unresolved Oedipal conflict in the relationship, an emotionally immature, dependent son and a close-binding, controlling mother, both mother and son are unlikely to achieve true spiritual freedom and healthy emotional independence.

Certain Oedipal echoes can be noted in the relationship of the priest and his brothers, usually taking the form of envy and jealousy. A priest-brother enjoys a patently unfair advantage in both the unconscious and conscious sibling rivalries that mark all but the healthiest of families. Even Jesus' chosen apostles wrestled with this lurking dynamic. James and John approach Jesus and ask to sit at his right and left when he comes into his glory. "And the other ten, on hearing this,

[17]John 2:5.

became indignant at James and John."[18] The prodigal son's older brother wallows in Oedipal envy and jealousy while his younger brother, motivated by the desire to break free of his father and family, has learned to be both grateful son and his own man.[19]

The Old Testament as well, studied from a post-Freudian point of view, exposes sinister inclinations and destructive, irrational behavior. Oedipal envy and rage overcome Cain and lead to the murder of his brother (Genesis 4). Rebekah conspires with her son, Jacob, to steal his brother Esau's birthright blessing (Genesis 27). Joseph suffers at the hands of his brothers (Genesis 37).[20] With little effort we observe envy and jealousy, rage and hatred, demonic self-seeking and ruthless competition, as threads weaving the very fabric of human history, as warring elements with heroic faith and self-sacrificing love in the narratives of sacred Scripture.

It is Jesus himself and the Gospel the priest is called to preach that uncover the paradoxical path to that inner freedom which follows upon Oedipal resolution.

> Jesus summoned them and said to them: "You know that those who are recognized as rulers over the Gentiles lord it over them, and their great ones make their authority over them felt. But it shall not be so among you. Rather, whoever wishes to be great among you will be your servant; whoever wishes to be first among you will be the slave of all. For the Son of Man did not come to be served but to serve and to give his life as a ransom for many."[21]

Freed from the burden of striving to be special, to be first in the eyes of his mother and father, his bishop and brother priests, the priest surrenders to the mystery of God's love for him, unearned, unmerited. Freed from the negative pull of Oedipal drives, he tastes the freedom of spiritual liberation. He walks now a man "at God's hand," supported and sustained by the peace of Christ.[22]

[18] Mark 10:35-41.

[19] Luke 15:11-32.

[20] See Cain Hope Felder, *Troubling Biblical Waters: Race, Class, and Family* (Maryknoll, N.Y.: Orbis Books, 1989) 151–52. See also Charles B. Copher, "The Black Presence in the Old Testament" in *Stony the Road We Trod: African American Biblical Interpretation,* ed. Cain Hope Felder (Minneapolis: Fortress Press, 1991) 146–53 and Helmut Schoeck, *Envy: A Theory of Social Behaviour* (Indianapolis: Liberty Fund, 1966).

[21] Mark 10:42-45.

[22] See "Edith Stein: Called to the Truth—Blessed by the Cross," a talk originally delivered by Friedrich Cardinal Wetter in the cathedral of Mainz, Germany, on February 7, 1984, trans. Josephine Koeppel, O.C.D., published by the Washington Province of Discalced Carmelites, Inc., 1998. Stein writes, "Basically, I have always only a small, simple truth to tell: how one can begin to live at God's hand."

Some Final, Oedipal Ruminations

The author and poet Kathleen Norris has observed: "A writer, whose name I have forgotten, once said that the true religions of America are optimism and denial."[23] There is, it seems, a cheery, shallow optimism that can be detected in certain circles of American society. It reveals in turn a cheery, shallow spirituality. For the optimism of our anonymous writer is not grounded in our liberating covenant with the Creator, with our salvation and redemption in Christ Jesus, nor is it sustained by the inspiring, life-giving passion of the Spirit. Rather, its roots can be traced to the false securities of secular-humanist thought. It is the whistling in the dark of the nominal believer whose American, practical approach to religion and life is, in the end, more profane than sacred. This American religion of optimism, upon inspection, is also a religion of denial. Denied and repressed are the unseemly ambitions that lead to domination and self-seeking. America's magnanimity as a nation and the fair-mindedness of her citizens coalesce into a state of soul unwilling to see its own injustice and sin. The twin religions of optimism and denial unfailingly lead to a blinding self-righteousness which in turn fosters resentment and envy in others. To the extent that optimism and denial take over the religious function of the soul, the soul displays the bravado of unresolved Oedipal conflict that simply cannot accept a defining dependency on the divine, on the profound relationality of life.

The gravest error of a civil religion built upon optimism and denial, however, is that it fails to take seriously the relentless pull in the human psyche to be "the only kid on the block." It fails to take evil seriously. It underestimates our fallen, i.e., Oedipal condition. It underestimates the destructive force of envy and rage, of the insatiable thirst to be unique and special, that dwells, at least in potency, in the breast of every man and woman. And it overestimates the glamor of power and status. This kind of false optimism holds to a sustaining hope that anyone can achieve the success enjoyed by the wealthy and beautiful people, and that all of this is what really matters.

A strikingly similar phenomenon can be observed in priests who have not yet discovered how to relate as an adult son to their parents, especially their mothers, and, at the same time, have not yet addressed the Oedipal forces at work in their relationship with their bishop. They ride a shallow optimism sustained by their denial of the psychic, unconscious dimensions to the priesthood while paying little atten-

---

[23]Kathleen Norris, *Cloister Walk* (New York: Riverhead Books, 1996) 94.

tion if any to the unconscious dimensions of the lives of their parishioners. These priests tend to spiritualize the mix of good and evil, success and failure, happiness and sorrow that daily touch their lives. They would have little patience with the following analysis of psychiatrist and spiritual mentor Gerald May:

> Searching beneath anxiety, one will find fear. And beneath fear hurt will be discovered. Beneath the hurt will be guilt. Beneath the guilt lie rage and hatred. But do not stop with this, for beneath the rage lies frustrated desire. Finally, beneath and beyond desire is love. In every feeling, look deeply. Explore without ceasing. At bottom, love is. Realizing this, Need one do anything about the anxiety one feels?[24]

Their ministry, untroubled by theological reflection, deprives their spirituality of depth, their pastoral care of genuine concern, their preaching of passion. They refuse to acknowledge their resentment at the achievements of their brother priests, but the very impugning of their peer's motives gives them away. Often, with underdeveloped priests, only the pseudo-comforts of clerical privilege distract them from their restlessness of soul. A growing resentment characterizes their relationships with authority (their bishops) and chronic irritability with their parishioners. Fatigue, loneliness, and a certain "psychic numbness"[25] make them prone to alcohol abuse and boundary violations.

On the other hand, priests willing to face the unconscious find a certain liberation in their acceptance of the not-always-apparent motives which fuel their ministry as servant-leaders. The iconic Oedipal drama will sooner or later lead them into a complex web of emotions that, once named, may be faced with compassion and courage. Their spiritual freedom infuses their preaching and teaching, their counseling and pastoral visits. Aware of the psychological and spiritual land mines dotting the priestly landscape, they are not surprised at the inevitable tensions that readily surface in their relationships with their bishop, brother priests, parishioners—and especially with the Church, herself. Naming these hidden forces somehow tends to disarm them.

Gradually the priest comes to understand that he must live out his vocation under the twin banners of fidelity and integrity. His salvation lies in being both a man of the Church and his own man. Freed from the shackles of Oedipal self-centeredness, the transparency of his soul reflects without refraction the light and love of God. His spiritual

[24]Gerald May, *Simply Sane* (New York: Crossroad, 1993) 87.

[25]Robert Jay Lifton, "The Sense of Immortality: On Death and the Continuity of Life," *Explorations of Psychohistory,* ed. R. Lifton and E. Olson (New York: Simon and Schuster, 1974) 282.

power is staggering for it is none other than the power of Jesus Christ, living in him.

Our discussion of Freud's Oedipal complex from the iconic or metaphoric perspective leaves us with an interesting corollary. If the Oedipal drama is at the core of our psychic reality, then we not only have "the complex," we *are* Oedipus. Wounded, confused, blinded, capable of every manner of evil, we priests stumble about for the light of the truth. As our blindness is overcome, we finally see that we not only commit sin—we are sin. Sin, Oedipal self-centeredness, is in our bones so to speak. Another truth becomes clear: if we are sin we are also grace. We boast with the saints and mystics that God now lives in us and we live in God. A meditation speaks to this reality:

> Lord God, have pity on me,
> for I am sin.
>
> I confess that I am human
>   of the earth, of the soil,
>   yet destined to fly and sail the winds.
>
> I confess the sin of idolatry.
>   I take myself too seriously.
>
> My ego-self I name Monarch.
>   I bow to the altar of my will,
>   I chafe at the will of others.
>
> I confess that I do not dance.
>   The cosmic dance is too dangerous,
>   the personal dance is too revealing.
>
> I confess that I do not laugh with abandonment.
>   My fragile ego permits only tight-lipped smiles.
>
> I confess my vanity, my pride turned inside out.
>   My dignity disdains the freedom of the foolish.
>
> I confess my fear, my anxiety, my docility.
>   My fear is sin; it masks my lack of faith.
>   My anxiety is betrayal; it reveals my lack of hope.
>   My docility is deference; it exposes my fear of freedom.
>
> I confess my respectability.
>   I place propriety ahead of spontaneity and freedom.
>
> Lord, God, have pity on me,
> for I am sin.

* * *

Lord, God, have pity on me,
for I am grace.

In your grace I am born again
and transformed
and made new.

Though I hardly know the depth of my sin,
it is touched and embraced,
it is soothed with the oil of forgiveness,
with the balm of mercy.

My darkness you overcome,
My guilt you lift,
My anxiety you still.

I confess that I am sin.
I confess that I am grace.

In my sin,
In your grace,
I confess that you are God.

And in sin and grace
I remain your beloved friend.[26]

In the light of God's unspeakable mercy and love, we no longer desire to be "the only kid on the block." We take our place among the "friends of God and prophets."[27] The Oedipal shadows dissolve. In the new light, the priest stands free and humble—an instrument, a servant, a living sacrament of divine grace and mercy.

[26]Donald B. Cozzens, "Confession," *Emmanuel,* vol. 92, no. 5 (June 1986) 270–71.

[27]See Elizabeth Johnson, *Friends of God and Prophets* (New York: Continuum, 1998). Johnson's brilliant retrieval of the communion of saints points to the surest path I have found out of the Oedipal thicket of solipsistic yearning. In this holy communion of God's friends and prophets, soul and psyche find liberation and redemption.

5

Becoming a Man

Take your life in your own
hands and what happens?
A terrible thing: no one to blame.

—Erica Jong

Maturity is disillusionment into wisdom.

—Ernest Becker

A man must go on a quest
to discover the sacred fire
in the sanctuary of his own belly
to ignite the flame in his heart
to fuel the blaze in the hearth
to rekindle his ardor for the earth

—Sam Keen

"The drug dealer, the ducking and diving political leader, the wife beater, the chronically 'crabby' boss, the 'hot shot' junior executive, the unfaithful husband, the company 'yes man,' the indifferent graduate school adviser, the 'holier than thou' minister, the gang member . . . all these men have something in common. They are all boys pretending to be men."[1] Real men make the best priests and a great many of them constitute the backbones of presbyterates from coast to coast. Their moral courage and spiritual strength are well known to their brother priests and close friends. They carry their masculine maturity easily, effortlessly. Like all mature adults, their integrity has been

[1]Robert Moore and Douglas Gillette, *King, Warrior, Magician, Lover: Rediscovering the Archetypes of the Mature Masculine* (San Francisco: Harper, 1990) 13.

tested time and again and they have stood their ground. Some priests, however, remain "boys pretending to be men." What keeps these priests from realizing their masculine maturity in Christ?

Vestiges of Oedipal conflict, we have seen, linger on in the depths of the psyche resisting the more or less definitive resolution found in individuals who have reached significant maturity in matters of the heart and soul. Integrated, emotionally mature people have, for the most part, moved beyond the insidious pull of envy and self-absorption. Their maturity and soulful living reflect the peace that is different from the world's peace. Many, however, including some priests, stand outside this circle of maturity. Original sin, that fundamental flaw and the great wound of the human soul, programs priest and layperson alike to subtly deny their dependent creature-hood and to enter into the self-defeating struggle to be the center of our world, the "apple of our mother's eye," the favored son (daughter) of the father—and in the deeper recesses of the soul, to be creator rather than creature.

Where priests have turned away from the soul work necessary to attend to either family of origin or ecclesial Oedipal conflict, they find themselves bereft not only of spiritual freedom but also of authenticity. Their restricted souls simply do not ring true. Quirks of character common to adolescents—pettiness, resentment, restlessness, willfulness—tend to undermine the efficacy of their ministry while leaving them dissatisfied and unfulfilled. From a developmental perspective, priests caught in this bind need to grow up. They need to become men. Not the pseudo-manliness associated with the aggressive, self-centered male of American culture, but the manliness of the self-possessed, self-confident male whose inner strength of character transcends body-image and other markers of the macho male. Becoming a man, becoming a woman, is essentially a matter of becoming the person, male or female, that God has destined one to be.

Obstacles to Manhood

The discipline of the pre-conciliar seminary rivaled that of a strict monastery and often approached the discipline of a military academy. While encouraging a certain thickness of skin, a certain spiritual toughness, it was not particularly successful in shaping emotionally mature men. Church leaders of that period seemed to assume that the common life of the seminary and the demands of a rather rigorous academic formation promoted both spiritual and emotional maturity. Critical thinking and probing questions were seldom encouraged while virtues such as docility and deference, coupled with a cheerful, upbeat yet passive piety, were affirmed and rewarded.

The post-conciliar seminary is significantly ahead of the pre-conciliar seminary in its understanding of the dynamics that foster authentic, mature human development. Yet the sobering realities of marriage, fatherhood, and mortgage that often shake an emotionally adolescent male into maturity and manhood remain, with growing exceptions, outside the experience of the seminarian and priest. In addition, the common social markers of maturity and success—a professional salary, a home or condominium—are simply not of the priest's world. Instead, he enjoys unprecedented job security and a salary less than a custodian's. Room and board, of course, are supplied by the parish. While most priests today lead quite comfortable lives with many of the same amenities of their affluent parishioners, they are "taken care of" by the Church. A certain liberation from financial anxiety follows upon this situation and most priests, I believe, appreciate not having to worry about money. But the psychological implications of being "taken care of" well into one's thirties and beyond are often overlooked. According to Robert Hovda, "Clergy and other professional servants of the churches are kept in a state of economic serfdom and dependency on fringe benefits, sycophancy and tax evasion, discouraging the very freedom, independence and maturity we are finally beginning to desire in our ministers."[2]

A certain sense of false security, then, buoys the priest up as long as he is loyal to this mother Church which provides for him, takes care of him. Should he be perceived as disloyal, however, his security is displaced by shame. Underneath the good life of clerical culture, healthy priests notice twinges of existential guilt. Frightened of the risks involved in personal authenticity and independence, some choose to remain, in Michael Crosby's words, "prisoners of privilege."[3] To the extent that a priest succumbs to the privileged comforts and perks of the clerical lifestyle, he is faced with the task of rationalizing his compromised authenticity. Often the relentless demands of pastoral ministry leave little time or energy for the kind of soulful reflection needed to see the shadow side of his world. The pace of parish life, the endless cycle of meetings and pastoral visits, the wakes and funerals, the administrative

[2]Robert Hovda, "Money or Gifts for the Poor and the Church," The Amen Corner: *Worship*, vol. 59, no. 1, 1985, 70–71.

[3]For a sustained discussion of the spiritual and psychological effects of clericalism, see Michael H. Crosby's *Celibacy: Means of Control or Mandate of the Heart?* (Notre Dame, Ind.: Ave Maria Press, 1996).

and financial responsibilities, make it easy to ignore the vague, "something's wrong" feeling of existential guilt. He begins to live in a state of "half-obscurity" about his own condition.[4] Trapped and tired, his spiritual pilgrimage toward emotional maturity and adult freedom is easily side-tracked. Should this be the case, his very manhood is at stake.

The Shaman or Priest Archetype

Jungian psychologist Terrance McBride has noted that "In the unconscious of all priests there is an archetype of priesthood, which . . . they ignore at their own peril, for it belongs to their life, it is part of their destiny."[5] Addressing the Jungian concept of archetype, William Perri, priest and psychotherapist, writes, "archetypes are the *Imago Dei*, the image of God, in a soul; the primordial forms that have existed since the remotest times. The archetype of priesthood can be traced as far back as the beginnings of human civilization, far in advance of Christianity. These primordial patterns are universal forms of behavior, centers of energy for the human psyche."[6] Jung held that archetypes were universal motifs, psychic patterns of affect and behavior.[7] Thus, archetypal psychology makes a significant contribution to a rather impoverished Catholic theology of vocation.

Considering that among the archetypes are mother, father, teacher, healer, magician, warrior, hero, heroine, and shaman or priest, individuals whose personal unconscious coincides with an archetypal pattern of the collective unconscious experience an inclination, a pull, a call (vocation) to the social role corresponding to the archetype. A woman, for example, who acknowledges that she always wanted to be a doctor may well be responding to the psychic influence of the healer archetype. In that case, her personal "truth" includes the identity of physician. From an archetypal psychology perspective, her career in medicine is much more than an arbitrary choice based on whim, social

---

[4]Soren Kierkegaard, *The Sickness Unto Death,* 1849 (Anchor ed., 1954, combined with *Fear and Trembling,* trans. Walter Lowrie) 181.

[5]Terrance McBride, "Catholicism and Jungian Psychology," *Catholicism and Jungian Psychology,* ed. J. Marvin Spiegelman (Phoenix: Falcon Press, 1988) 187, quoted in William D. Perri, *A Radical Challenge for Priesthood Today* (Mystic, Conn.: Twenty-Third Publications, 1996) 10.

[6]William D. Perri, *A Radical Challenge for Priesthood Today,* 11. Perri's work deserves serious attention from bishops, priests, and individuals struggling to understand the crisis gripping the soul of the priest.

[7]C. G. Jung, *The Archetypes of the Collective Unconscious,* Bollingen Series, XX, vol. 9, part 1 (Princeton, N.J.: Princeton University Press, 1959, 1969) 3–41.

status, anticipated financial rewards, or even a desire to do something meaningful with her life.

A vocation to the priesthood may have a similar archetypal component. In like fashion, the grace of a vocation may well build on the natural psychic predisposition for priestly ministry that is constituted by the shaman or priest archetype. In this light, from both psychological and theological perspectives, a true vocation to service as a priest becomes the "truth" of the presbyter. He has been anointed, marked, if you will, for ministry as a priest. His desire for priesthood, then, is more than a career choice, even one based on the conscious motivation to do something worthwhile with his life. His vocation is cradled in a dialectic of grace building on nature (archetypal predisposition) and his response in faith to the mysterious promptings of his soul which are affirmed by the consensus of the local church and confirmed by the call of the diocesan bishop. He turns from this calling, therefore, with the possibility of facing real psychic and spiritual danger. McBride's warning bears repeating here. "In the unconscious of all priests is an archetype of priesthood, which . . . they ignore at their own peril, for it belongs to their life, it is part of their destiny."[8]

The *Puer Aeternus* Archetype

If the shaman or priest archetype constitutes a psychological predisposition for the priestly calling, another archetypal force can be observed in the personalities of a good number of priests: the *puer aeternus*—the eternal boy, the eternal youth.[9] Archetypal psychology,

---

[8]Terrance McBride suggests in "Catholicism and Jungian Psychology" in Spiegelman's *Catholicism and Jungian Psychology*, that "the idea of an indelible mark in the soul could correspond to a kind of priestly archetype or primordial imprint of what priesthood has always meant to human beings, being present in the psyche of certain people. Perhaps ordination could be seen as publicly recognizing this archetypal constellation in the person" (184).

[9]Marie-Louise von Franz, *Puer Aeternus* (Santa Monica, Calf.: Sigo Press, 1981). Von Franz, perhaps Carl Jung's closest professional confidante and friend, writes:

> *Puer aeternus* is the name of a god of antiquity. The words themselves come from Ovid's *Metamorphoses* and are there applied to the child-god in the Eleusinian mysteries. Ovid speaks of the child-god Iacchus, addressing him as *puer aeternus* and praising him in his role in these mysteries. In later times, the child-god was identified with Dionysus and the god Eros. He is the divine youth who is born in the night in this typical mother-cult mystery of Eleusis, and who is a redeemer. He is a god of life, death and resurrection—the god of divine youth. . . . The title *puer aeternus* therefore means "eternal

when focused on the personality and psychic makeup of priests, reveals an interesting phenomenon—the *puer* archetype appears to twin with the priest/shaman archetype in a good number of priests. Consider the typical *puer* characteristics: youthful enthusiasm, a kind of virginal innocence, a natural inclination for religion and ritual, the winsome charm linked to spiritual transparency—all qualities common not only to the shrinking number of presbyters under age forty but also to priests who have moved well into their middle years and beyond.

Priests, like women religious, tend to age well. It is not uncommon for siblings to tease their priest brother that he carries his years well because he lives a life remarkably free of the burdens and pressures of life and work in the "real world." Whether due to living well, the meaningfulness associated with pastoral ministry, the absence of anxieties relating to family, work, and life in the suburbs, or to the influence of the *puer* archetype, many priests project an aura of spiritual vitality and youthfulness of spirit. *Pueri*, generally speaking, tend to be appealing, approachable individuals who enjoy social mixing and easy conversation. Their youthful spirit, for the most part, contributes to a *persona* that is both attractive and arresting. Typically, they possess what Jungian psychology calls a numinous, i.e., spiritual, quality coupled with an innate innocence that seem particularly suited to the social role of the priest.

There is, as we might suspect, a negative side to the *puer* archetype. Under its influence, men tend to remain "too long in adolescent psychology; that is, all those characteristics that are normal in a youth of seventeen or eighteen are continued into later life, coupled in most cases with too great a dependence on the mother."[10] Often the only unmarried son, priests tend to have deep and tender relationships with their mothers. Edifying to parishioners and others who become aware of the priest-son's devotion, the relationship is regularly reinforced by queries to the priest about the well-being of his mother. Middle-aged and older priests regularly inquire about the health of their priest-friends' mothers. Both mother and priest-son find emotional support and consolation in one of nature's most complex, intimate relationships. While many, if not most, of these priest-mother relationships reflect the best of filial piety and healthy maternal love, some give clear

---

youth," but we also use it to indicate a certain type of young man who has an outstanding mother complex . . . (1).

See also James Hillman, ed., *Puer Papers* (Dallas: Spring Publications, 2nd printing, 1987), especially James Baird, "Puer Aeternus: The Figure of Innocence in Melville," 205–23.

[10]Marie-Louise von Franz, *Puer Aeternus*, 1.

evidence of being dysfunctional. When this is the case, the priest remains under the controlling will of his mother and the mother, failing to encourage a healthy independence in her son, remains overly dependent on him to meet her emotional needs. The priest, clearly an adult son, feels smothered and trapped, unduly influenced by the likes and whims of his mother, much like an adolescent son might feel as he moves toward a sense of manhood.

It is not uncommon for some mothers of priests to build their primary identity on their status as a "mother of a priest." Should this special mother-son relationship become too close-binding, too dependent, too controlling, the *puer* character to the priest's personality is easily reinforced. Well into his adult years, his mother's wishes and judgments influence him far beyond what is healthy and normal. A number of years ago, I heard a priest client report the following dream:

> It was the middle of the night, I was standing, naked and without embarrassment, in the enclosed courtyard of a Spanish-like home in the southwest. It was a warm, still night and I felt a sense of healing communion with its power and darkness, and with the earth's natural energy. In this state of harmony between spirit and nature, I felt the urge to urinate. And in the privacy of the enclosed space, I did. From the shadows, came the stern, shaming voice of my mother, "Nicolas! What are you doing?"

The primordial quality of the dream troubled him as he sensed its Oedipal, mother-complex character.

A man needs to leave home to become fully a man. The rite of passage takes different forms and is repeated as a young man moves into adulthood—leaving for college, joining the military, moving to another city for work, and, especially, marrying a wife, the most definitive of leave-taking. The priest, too, leaves home when he enters the seminary. Often the mother-complex finds a healthy resolution at this time. The seminary, however, is a kind of antechamber to the home he will find in the Church as a priest. Sometimes a seminarian finds in this antechamber even more security and comfort than he found in his family home. If he follows the rules, pleases his ecclesial "parents," he will be taken care of. He will be clothed in special robes, given an identity, enhanced with status, provided with leisure for prayer, study, and recreation, and exposed to the arts. Anxiety about earning a living, paying off a mortgage, raising a family—all this he will be spared. And if he is docile and shrewd, he may find himself in a special place of honor in this second home.

In spite of this potential danger for succumbing to a kind of ecclesial mother-complex, it is clear that many real men walk the halls of our seminaries and dwell as fully mature adults in the rectories of our Church. Having navigated the psychic currents of their natural homes, they draw upon the developmental lessons they learned growing up to navigate the psychic currents of their ecclesial home. They have discovered true fidelity to the Gospel and loyalty to the Church while remaining their own men. Their dependence upon mother-Church is appropriate and adult. Their deference to father-bishop is likewise appropriate and manly. Their spiritual depth and inner freedom have overcome any *puer* tendencies to adolescent self-centeredness and immaturity. There is no escaping, however, this spiritual and psychic test. Sooner or later, the priest's spiritual journey leads him to moments of truth where he is faced with the acutely uncomfortable tension of holding to the reality of his own pastoral experience as a man when that experience is in conflict with an ecclesial policy or non-dogmatic church teaching. These and similar defining moments test his mettle as a man. Something central to his soul and manhood is lost if he surrenders in these moments to denial and distraction.

Marie-Louise von Franz identifies two typical disturbances to the *puer* with an unresolved mother complex: homosexuality and Don Juanism, the psychological inability to make a serious, life-long commitment to a woman resulting in numerous superficial, romantic relationships of relatively short duration.[11] Here, the image of mother, the perfect woman to his unconscious, exaggerates the shortcomings and limitations found in the best of women and he simply cannot get beyond them. Each time he meets a woman to whom he is initially attracted, he eventually discovers that she is, in one way or another, imperfect; his unconscious radar unfailingly noting, with self-inflated righteousness, faults, weaknesses, or other blemishes that make her unacceptable.[12]

Spiritual directors and therapists who work with clergy regularly see priests, both heterosexual and homosexual in orientation, who evidence Don Juanism in their search for intimate friendship. Restless and

[11]C. G. Jung, *Symbols of Transformation, Collected Works*, vol. 5 (Princeton, N.J.: Princeton University Press, 1956; 2nd ed. 1967) par., 527.

[12]See Marie-Louise von Franz, *Puer Aeternus*. Von Franz believes

that he is looking for a mother goddess, so that each time he is fascinated by a woman he has later to discover that she is an ordinary human being. Having lived with her sexually, the whole fascination vanishes and he turns away disappointed, only to project the image anew onto one woman after another. He eternally longs for the maternal woman who will enfold him in her arms and satisfy his every need. This is often accompanied by the romantic attitude of the adolescent (2).

impatient, often displaying signs of a savior or messiah complex, they search with youthful idealism for the perfect intimate friend. Often charming and attractive themselves, they leave trails of wounded, hurt individuals upon whom they have lavished their interest and attention— for a time. The emotional pain they cause is considerable.

For some priests, coming into emotional maturity concurs with being named to their first pastorate. The responsibility, the work and the worry of it, tend to dissolve residual *puer* qualities in their personalities. Especially the work involved with an appointment to a pastorate can be helpful to the *puer* priest. For *pueri* have serious difficulty with work. Should a task hold a special fascination for the "eternal youth," he will throw himself into it. But even creative, interesting work has its routine and pedestrian moments. Sooner or later, his inability to stay with the task until it is completed becomes a serious bone of contention with his pastoral colleagues. Most of the parish, however, cannot see this weakness in the priest. What they do see is a pleasant, friendly, young-in-spirit parish priest. Interestingly, Jung and von Franz see no other cure for the negative aspects of the *puer* archetype than a serious, sustained commitment to work.[13]

The capacity and discipline for sustained work that is not always pleasant is one of the marks of a mature person. Obviously, the dignity and nature of priestly ministry, the complexity and responsibility of it, requires adult maturity. From the time of ordination, the priest is charged with preaching the word of God, living that word in such a fashion that he preaches with his very life. From a human point of view, only the spiritually and emotionally mature can make the word of God a living, saving force in others. Pastoring, not for the faint of heart, is equally ill-suited for the lazy of soul; it is for the adult leader purified in the discipline of the cross. The priest is called to be such a leader— he is called to be innocent without being naïve, committed without being aloof, a man of the Church without being clerical or elitist. Only the mature adult, full in the stature of grace, meets these demands.

Celibacy takes an interesting turn for the priest marked with the *puer* archetype. Instinctually drawn to marriage by his libido energy, the heterosexually oriented priest finds that its appeal remains generalized, seldom experiencing a prolonged attraction to an individual woman that he might want to marry. He can spot the features that make any given woman less than perfect, and thus unacceptable. His *puer* spirit remains too lofty for the everyday world of diapers and dishes; these mundane realities threaten to suffocate his soul, a soul

[13]Ibid., 5–6.

clearly fixed on the horizon, on the limitless possibilities for spiritual creativity and personal relationships—relationships that are delightful and intense but, for the most part, short-lived. Here the stage is set for the Don Juan feature commonly associated with the *puer* personality. Aware of a need for intimacy but not drawn specifically to marriage with any one woman, the priest-*puer* is captivated by the sweet undertones of eros and romance that he finds in his relationships with certain women, especially intelligent, naturally spiritual women. If the priest is conflicted by the forces of a mother complex, he may be particularly drawn to strong, controlling women. Often deep and exciting relationships are formed, technically chaste and celibate, that may last for months and, sometimes, for a year or so.

The true Don Juan priest finds emotional fulfillment and considerable affirmation in these friendships, for yet another woman finds him attractive and is perhaps "spiritually" in love with him. Women may easily overlook the serious immaturity behind the winsome *persona* of the "boy" priest. A woman, of course, involved in a friendship with a Don Juan–*puer* priest risks considerable emotional pain. It is not always easy to see the serious immaturity behind the winsome *persona* of the "boy" priest. The lack of mutual maturity tends to make for brief, intense relationships between a mature woman and a *puer* priest. At the same time, the grace of a friendship with a mature woman often proves to be the priest's salvation. Her maturity, spirituality, and committed fidelity provide the security needed for the priest to face his own anxiety and fears. Understanding and accepting without judgment, she leads the *puer* priest out of his immature cloud of emotional unknowing into the freedom and authenticity of manhood.[14]

The homosexually oriented *puer* priest, not finding marriage appealing on any deep, existential level of his being, looks to clerical celibacy with a different kind of ambiguity than his heterosexual colleague. Luminous, lighthearted, and socially adept, other gay men find him attractive and desire his friendship. The immaturity inherent to the *puer* archetype, however, puts him at risk for unhealthy, exploitative relationships with gay men. At the same time, he might enjoy authentic, close, and uncomplicated relationships with women. We return to the issue of homosexually oriented priests in Chapter 7.

[14]Andrew Greeley's novels capture the redemptive role women often exercise in their relationships with priests.

A Few Weak Men

Priests today stand awash in a floodlight of suspicion in the eyes of contemporary American culture. Neither macho playboy nor successful careerist, they go about their work without wife and children, without a home of their own, without the cultural symbols that define achievement. In the eyes of many, their manliness drifts about in a sea of ambiguity, and recent clerical scandals of sexual misconduct with young boys have severely tarnished their collective reputation. They have lost their innocence. In Catholic circles, the priest still commands considerable respect and remains extraordinarily important to the majority of Catholics. But it is clearly not the same as it was in the halcyon days of the 1940s and 50s.

Jesuit theologian Michael Buckley, when serving as rector of The Jesuit School of Theology at Berkeley, proposed that what the Church needed in her priests were a few weak men. He asks of the seminarian ready to be ordained, "Is this man weak enough to be a priest?"[15] His question takes us back to the humanity and manhood of Christ who was judged a weak and ineffective leader of a religious movement comprised of discouraged and confused Jewish peasants, to the weakness of a stammering Peter, to the ambition of James and John. Buckley continues:

> Let me spell out what I mean. Is this man deficient enough so that he can't ward off significant suffering from his life, so that he lives with a certain amount of failure, so that he feels what it is to be an average man? Because it is in this deficiency, in this interior lack, in this weakness, maintains *Hebrews*, that the efficacy of the ministry and priesthood of Christ lies.[16]

Buckley's rhetorical question reminds us that the issue of manhood and priesthood has little in common with the various contemporary "men's movements" that surfaced in the 1990s.[17] It has everything to

[15]Michael Buckley, "A Letter to the Ordinands," *The Berkeley Jesuit* (Spring 1972) 8.

[16]Ibid.

[17]See Robert Bly, *Iron John* (Reading, Mass.: Addison-Wesley Publishing, 1990), and Sam Keen, *Fire in the Belly* (New York: Bantam Books, 1991) for two early proponents of the men's movements. Other works relating to the present chapter are: Patrick M. Arnold, *Wildmen, Warriors, and Kings: Masculine Spirituality and the Bible* (New York: Crossroad, 1991), and Moore and Gillette, *King, Warrior, Magician, Lover*. See also William Masters, Virginia Johnson, and Robert Kolodny, *Human Sexuality* (New York: Harper Collins, 1992) 278, as quoted in William D. Perri, op. cit., 82.

do, however, with reflecting the inner strength and maturity of Jesus the Christ. At the heart of the matter is the priest's authenticity and integrity, his freedom and quiet self-confidence. Only a priest who is fundamentally mature can lead with wisdom and steady strength. Only someone who has looked courageously into his wounded depths and faced his weakness "in Christ" can preach with conviction and passion.

6

Tending the Word

Spirit is very strange.
It has an obligation to create.

—Mircea Eliade

Imagination is evidence
of the Divine.

—William Blake

Preach always.
When necessary, use words.

—Francis of Assisi

The imagination of the priest has been jostled in recent years to look afresh at his responsibility as a tender of the word. The jostling began in earnest with the conciliar fathers insisting that "priests . . . have as their primary duty the proclamation of the gospel of God to all"[1] and has been sustained by Paul VI's *Evangelii nuntiandi*.[2] Seminaries, schools of theology, and continuing education programs for priests have each addressed the challenge of forming effective homilists. Still, fundamental to the preaching of the word and transcending various approaches to homiletics training is the human formation of the preacher.[3] Effective preachers, then, are found among

[1]Walter M. Abbott, S.J., and Joseph Gallagher, eds. *"Presbyterorum ordinis,"* *The Documents of Vatican II* (New York: The America Press, 1966) no. 4, 538–39.

[2]Paul VI, *Evangelization in the Modern World,* Apostolic Exhortation, 197.

[3]John Paul II, *I Will Give You Shepherds (Pastores dabo vobis)*, Post-synodal Apostolic Exhortation, March 25, 1992, Propositio 21, "The whole work of priestly formation would be deprived of its necessary foundation if it lacked a suitable human formation," 116–17.

those mature individuals who are counted, because of their wisdom, spirituality, and common sense, as elders of the Church. They are men and women who believe deeply and with passion.

In the case of the priest, who is commissioned to make preaching his primary ministry, the desire to tend to the word with reverence and imagination should be evident to all. While a pilgrim with other believers, his sense of himself as a man and a priest disposes the congregation to listen for a word from the Lord. It should be clear that he himself has humbly listened for a word from the Lord. In his personal tending to the word his identity as a priest comes into focus. It is in the power of this word that he finds the courage to remain faithfully a man of the Church while remaining his own person.

Capable of honest, intimate friendship, the priest-tender of the word will unselfconsciously communicate that he understands both the joy and pain of loving with fidelity and trust. The sacrament of his own humanity will speak without words the predisposing truth that he has stood in the fire of human trial and emerged tried and true. A redeemed sinner, he will drink daily from the chalice of mercy and begin anew to be a living icon of Jesus Christ. Like tenders of the bar, he stands waiting to serve the "waters of life" that ease the burdens of life and labor. Unlike the bartender, however, he both waits to serve and takes bold action to bring the living word of God, the bread of life, and the cup of salvation to the hungry, thirsty, and lost.

In the process of faithfully tending to the word, the priest discovers that he is also tending to his own soul. More to the core of his mission, tending the word is the purest form of tending to the people of his parish. Saved himself by this word, he swallows and dares to do what he was ordained to do, he dares to preach.

Too often, it seems to me, the priest dares to preach alone. An easy enough thing to do; he stands at the ambo by himself, after all. In so doing, sooner or later he reveals the depth or shallowness of his soul. Is there anything more alone one can do in a liturgical setting? Even singing the *Exsultet* at the Easter Vigil is less revealing. In a real sense, nonetheless, the priest doesn't preach alone. He draws courage and inspiration from all who preach in the name of the Lord. Something is lost if the priest forgets that he is one of a company of preachers, linked with the bishop, presbyters, and deacons of his local church, and sharing in their common mission to be tenders of the word. He is linked, furthermore, to the company of preachers that go well beyond the boundaries of his diocese—to those men and women anointed by God's spirit and affirmed by ecclesial authority to preach God's liberating, saving word.

Preachers, I suspect, tend to forget that they share a common anointing as tenders of the word. As such they are meant to encourage one another, to draw strength and inspiration from each other, and to hold each other in prayer and affection. Priests who meet regularly with other preachers to prepare for the Sunday homily are quick to acknowledge the benefit of shared preparation: an awakened sacramental imagination; a broader exegetical horizon; particular events or factors affecting the local church; appropriate stories that resonate with the readings. As preachers meet to discuss the assigned Scripture readings and their personal approaches to the homily, they cannot help but engage in what has come to be known as *faith sharing* and *life sharing*. In this common tending to the word they find themselves tended by the word itself.

A Spirituality of the Word

Tending the word, it should be clear by now, is at the core of the priest's spirituality. To him the word has been entrusted. Karl Rahner notes that: "This efficacious word has been entrusted to the priest. To him has been given the word of God. That makes him a priest."[4] A presbyteral spirituality, then, that is not grounded in the saving word of God and in tending to this word will lack the depth and power of the word itself.

Abraham Heschel captured the essence of this intimate relationship between word and spirit when he claimed that he preached in order to pray.[5] Prayer, of course, must precede preaching the word of God, for preaching is alive only if it flows from the preacher's spiritual core, a spiritual core nourished and sustained by prayer and an abiding state of prayerfulness. Yet, Heschel's insight is critical. He preached in order to pray. If a priest's preaching does not prompt him to pray, at least most of the time, something is amiss in his soul. Those who tend to the word through preaching find a quiet but insistent pull to solitude welling up within them after they have preached. Preaching, Heschel argues, is "successful" when it leads the assembly to prayer.[6]

---

[4]Karl Rahner, "Priest and Poet," *Theological Investigations,* vol. 3, trans. Karl-H. Kruger and Boniface Kruger (New York: Helicon, 1967) 303.

[5]Abraham Joshua Heschel, *Quest for God: Studies in Prayer and Symbolism* (New York: Crossroad, 1982). Heschel writes, "Preach in order to pray. Preach in order to inspire others to pray. The test of a true sermon is that it can be converted to prayer" (80).

[6]Ibid.

The homily then, that holy tending of the word that is the staff of the ministerial priesthood, becomes the ground and center of the priest's spirituality—especially, we shall see, of the parish priest's spirituality. For the parish priest, at the prompting of the council, now preaches at weekday Eucharist as well as the vigil and Sunday celebrations of Mass.[7] Fidelity to this responsibility and privilege inevitably leads to prayer. In light of his calling to be a tender of the word, the priest's decision to pray is arguably the most important decision he can make.[8]

Without a decisive commitment to prayer, the ministry of preaching at Sunday and daily liturgies becomes an intolerable burden to the priest—and to those who hear him. Rather than tending to the word, the spiritually shallow priest subverts the word. With unusual passion, Rahner insists that

> the word of God in the mouth of a priest empty of faith and love is a judgment more terrible than all versification and all poetic chatter in the mouth of a poet who is not really one. It is already a lie and a judgment upon a man, if he speaks what is not in him; how much more, if he speaks of God while he is godless.[9]

Faithful to prayer and *lectio divina,* to the quiet listening for the voice of God as revealed to him in the events of the day, the tending of the word becomes the priest's rock of salvation, the cornerstone of his spiritual life.

The Art of Preaching

While fidelity to the word, tending the word through preaching, teaching, and prayer are clearly central to the pastoral mission of the priest, research reveals a general dissatisfaction among U.S. Catholics with the quality of the homilies they hear Sunday after Sunday. Certainly, the very quantity of preaching events the typical parish priest faces in the course of the week is a factor. In addition to the weekday and weekend eucharistic liturgies, he preaches at funerals, weddings, and special school Masses among others, which is without

---

[7]Walter M. Abbott, S.J., and Joseph Gallagher, eds., *"Sacrosanctum concilium," The Documents of Vatican II,* no. 52. "The homily . . . is to be highly esteemed as a part of the liturgy itself. . ." (55).

[8]See Donald B. Cozzens, "Tenders of the Word," in Donald B. Cozzens, ed., *The Spirituality of the Diocesan Priest* (Collegeville: The Liturgical Press, 1997) 50ff.

[9]Rahner, "Priest and Poet," *Theological Investigations,* vol. 3, 308.

question a heavy burden to the most prayerful and reflective priest. Other factors, however, seem to be at play. It is possible that the priest believes that the very power and truth of the word he preaches by itself will convince and convict his listeners. His task, he believes, is to present this word without ambiguity and then to apply it to the lives of the congregation: the typical "exegesis and lettuce" sermon.

Paul Tillich once observed that the fundamental mistake preachers and teachers make is to communicate the truth of the Gospel without first eliciting in the minds of their hearers the implicit question or questions to which the truth offers at least some partial answer. Tillich held that the sermon first needs to address the ambiguity, pain, and privilege of the human condition. How is it, the preacher might ask, that we can feel alienation when in the company of family and those who love us? Why do we feel, at least at times, so wondrously blessed even when our brokenness and sinfulness tend to overwhelm us? How can we cope, not to mention make some sense, out of human suffering and tragedy? Why do we tend to hurt the very ones we love?

Addressing these and similar questions first, Tillich insists, awakens a thirst for the healing power and truth of God's word. The heart, so to speak, leans forward, straining to hear a consoling and challenging word from the Lord. Something serious is lost if this dialectic between existential question (the human condition) and essential answer (the word of God) is not sustained in our preaching and religious education. Of course, God's word does not fully answer our human questions, but the story of God's saving presence in human history is the story of salvation and mercy. And behold, the story is told in this moment, and God's spirit visits us here and now.

Annie Dillard captured the word's potential to shake our very foundations when she wrote that

> It is madness to wear ladies' straw hats and velvet hats to church; we should all be wearing crash helmets. Ushers should issue life preservers and signal flares; they should lash us to our pews. For the sleeping god may wake someday and take offense, or the waking god may draw us out to where we can never return.[10]

If there is a crisis in preaching in the Church today, part of the solution can be found in the preacher's imagination. Mary Catherine Hilkert, in her seminal theology of preaching *Naming Grace*, describes the ministry of preaching as the art of "naming grace," the

---

[10]Annie Dillard, "Expedition to the Pole," in *Teaching a Stone to Talk* (New York: Harper and Row, 1982) 41.

grace of mercy and healing, the grace of forgiveness and reconciliation, the grace of life and love itself.[11]

The art of tending the word, quite understandably, begins with the craft of preparing the homily. The priest preacher sits in contemplative prayer, reflects upon the readings of the Sunday, searches for the existential questions that bear upon the Scriptures, allows his imagination room to work, and waits for the homily to rise into his consciousness from both heart and head. Invariably and sometimes quite spontaneously his words name the grace, the saving power of God that triumphs ultimately over the disgrace of human pride and fear, over all forms of sin. He discovers that often the best way to present the truth of Jesus Christ is through stories.

"Stories," insists Andrew Greeley, "have always been the best way to talk about religion because stories appeal to the emotions and the whole personality and not just to the mind."[12] Jesus' use of the parable arrested the imagination of his listeners and allowed him to bring home the most subversive and liberating truths without moralizing or pedantic preaching: the first shall be last and the last first; the prodigal son comes to his senses, the Samaritan's compassion shames that of the priest and Levite; the kingdom of God belongs to the humble and childlike. Yet, "cultural or religious stories," according to Hilkert, "can only function as preachings of the gospel if the preacher recognizes there a reflection of the specific gospel passage that is to be preached and makes those connections clear—whether explicitly or implicitly."[13] The skilled preacher therefore knows the power of story and how and when to use story in his or her preaching.

Tending as Evangelization

Essential to any spirituality and ministry grounded in the word of God is the responsibility to renew the face of the earth with the Gospel of Jesus Christ. The breadth and scope of this mission, however, places it among those grand ideals that both challenge our imagination and, from time to time, disturb our conscience. The chal-

[11]Mary Catherine Hilkert, *Naming Grace: Preaching and the Sacramental Imagination* (New York: Continuum, 1997) especially chapter 6, "The Human Story and the Story of Jesus," 89–107.

[12]Andrew M. Greeley, *The Cardinal Sins* (New York: Bernard Geis, 1982), from Greeley's afterword to the novel, 509.

[13]Mary Catherine Hilkert, "Parables of Grace," Keynote address, *Societas Homiletica, Conference on Preaching Grace in the Human Condition,* Washington, D.C., March 1, 1999.

lenge is so lofty, so sweeping, that it seems to carry its own dispensation from specific action. The passing guilt associated with this fundamental responsibility is similar to the voice of conscience when a priest judges himself more as a "guilty bystander" than an active agent in the work for peace and justice. Of course, priests do "proclaim the Gospel to all" in their local ministry to one or more parishes. They do work for justice and peace as servant leaders making real and honest efforts to feed the hungry and care for the homeless.

Often, the global vision of Paul VI's *Evangelii nuntiandi* fades into the background of the priest's consciousness as the demands of parish leadership consume his time and energy. Should this be the case, the narrowed intentionality that follows sets the priest up for psychic exhaustion. He and his coworkers in the vineyard are at risk for ministerial burn-out. The priest and other full time lay and religious ministers may miss a significant paradox: the broader the focus the lighter the load.

Years ago I came across a story I often use when preaching retreats to priests. It illustrates the importance of seeing the broad picture and intentionality's power to liberate our imagination. And where imagination goes, energy follows:

> A long time ago, on a sweltering, humid afternoon, a lone traveler leaves the security of a walled, medieval city. When just a mile or so from the city gate, he sees in the distance three men inching their way toward him, each pushing a wheelbarrow piled high with bricks. As the first man approaches, the traveler asks, "What are you doing?"
>
> Irritated at the rather needless question, the tired and thirsty man answers, "I'm pushing this wheelbarrow loaded with bricks!"
>
> As the second man draws near, he puts the same question to him. He receives, however, a different answer, "I have a wife and young children; they have to eat. And I have to work to feed them."
>
> Moving on to the third worker, he asks, "What are you doing?" He stops, lowers the handles of the wheelbarrow, and looks up at his questioner. In his eyes the traveler sees more than fatigue and weariness. He catches a hint of pride and dignity.
>
> "What am I doing? I'm building a cathedral!"

The differing grades of intentionality make the same tedious work quite different for the three laborers of the story. As the intentionality becomes more other-directed, it transcends the first order of perception—in this case, the unmediated hard work. The higher levels of intentionality evident in the second and third workers allow them to experience real meaningfulness and dignity in their labor as well as greater energy for the task at hand. Paul VI's apostolic letter offers priests and pastoral ministers the critical vision: their service to the word of God, no matter how local, is building the reign of God, one brick at a time. As bearers of the word, the burdens and heat of the day take their toll. If a priest takes up the burden of naming grace day in and day out, if he gives his heart and soul to the task, his blood will be in the bricks.

No matter what level of intentionality he brings to his work as a priest, unnerving questions will nevertheless disturb his rest. Does his preaching make a difference? His counseling, teaching, pastoral care— do they touch peoples' lives, turn peoples' hearts to God? The painful human limitations of the preacher, the fear and mistrust so evident in the curial offices of the Vatican, the sinfulness of the Church itself make it clear that the cathedral will never be completed during the preacher's life. The preacher, as bearer of the word, labors under a terrible illusion if he expects to see more than the ordinary miracles of grace that occur each day among the people he serves. At these times priests can take consolation in Paul VI's insistence that evangelists themselves need to be evangelized. Though tenders and bearers of the word, they need to hear what they dare to bring to others. Priests, I believe, can easily forget their need to hear the word of God. There is a time to tend the word and a time to listen to the word, and they remember as the word both soothes and challenges them that evangelists need to be evangelized.

The crises buffeting the souls of priests demand that they listen afresh, with open hearts and ready imagination, to the word broken and blessed, in many cases by their non-ordained pastoral associates when they preach at liturgies of the hours, at wake services, at parish retreats and renewals. At other times the word of God is spoken by the dying woman they anoint or the jailed man they visit, or the brave teenager dealing with the divorce of her parents. At those times they see what is often missed, that each member of their parish, each friend and family member, each member of the parish staff, literally everyone, is pushing a wheelbarrow filled with bricks. In this bearing of the cross of Christ, the reign of God silently unfolds in history.

It has been said that we mortals cannot stand to live a meaningless life.[14] More often than not priests speak of a desire to do something meaningful with their lives when trying to explain what led them to the priesthood. Say what you will, the priesthood remains

---

[14]Wallace Clift, *Jung and Christianity: The Challenge of Reconciliation* (New York: Crossroad, 1982).

one of the more meaningful ways of living and serving. As a tender of God's word, the priest is privileged to speak about what really matters and in doing so he becomes a mediator of meaning.[15]

By his life as well as his words, the priest points to the paradox of the beatitudes and the foolishness of the Gospel. If he himself knows what really matters, his preaching promises deliverance to those who are owned by their possessions and find, in the midst of the many things they own, nothing but emptiness. This kind of evangelizing demands that he see with the eye of the artist and listen with the ear of the poet. It demands commitment to solitude in order to hear what only the quiet heart can hear. Formed and purified by the word itself, he is ready to speak it boldly and well to his parishioners. In the prayer that follows his preaching, he sees with Bernano's country priest that "all is grace."

Resisting the Word

Tenders of the word must sit with God's word, savor it as a wine connoisseur savors a winery's prize vintage. He reads it slowly and carefully, letting it filter into the corners of his unconscious where it takes root under the quiet tutoring of his imagination. Here the word begins to reveal its ever-new promise to transform the lives of those who will soon hear it aloud from the preachers' lips. A certain anxiety surfaces as the preacher remembers Karl Barth's words, "Preaching is 'God's own word.' That is to say, through the activity of preaching, God himself speaks."[16]

The anxiety leads to the question: have I tended the word well enough, wrestled with its meaning long enough, studied the commentaries thoroughly enough to allow God to speak through me, the preacher? Priests who know their church history smile knowingly at the dangers inherent in preaching God's word. They know, for example, that three ecumenical councils and eleven popes condemned usury in the name of God's word. To hold otherwise was heresy which, in that period of the church's history, could lead to the stake. So, the preacher struggles to tell the truth. But to tell the truth one must see the truth, and the truth of God's word can be so unsettling that in every age preachers close their eyes to the full implications of the word they preach. Seldom is the failure fully culpable. The failure to see often

[15]See Donald Cozzens, "Bearer of the Word," *The Charism of the Priesthood*, vol. VII, no. 3 (National Federation of Priests' Councils, 1996) 17–21.

[16]Karl Barth, *The Preaching of the Gospel*, trans. B. E. Hooke (Philadelphia: Westminster, 1963) 54–55.

results from the force of the sustaining ecclesial and cultural structures that may compromise the radical character of God's word.

In every age the Spirit nudges the collective consciousness of the Church to see ever more clearly the radical new order of the gospel message. I thought of this point when I came across a letter, written over two hundred years ago, from Bishop John Carroll of Baltimore to the prioress of the Carmelite Sisters. The Carmelites had arrived in the Commonwealth of Maryland in 1790, settling in Port Tobacco. There the sisters maintained a small farm for over a generation before moving to Baltimore in 1831. The letter announced a gift from the bishop intended to ease the hardships of the sisters demanding life in the new world. The gift consisted of two slaves, a mother and her daughter.[17] Bishop Carroll and the Carmelite Sisters were bright and good people. Yet they did not see what we see clearly today. Two hundred years from now, our descendants will be puzzled at the blind spots of our present Church. They were good and wise people, it will be reasoned, why couldn't they see what we are able to see from this point in history?

Preachers know they will be judged by the very word they dare to preach. Some, it seems, may even lose their soul in their tending of the word. Without hope and on the edge of despair themselves, they preach an extravagant hope; blind or at least tolerant of injustice within the Church, they preach justice and peace to their congregations and to the world; unloving themselves, they nevertheless demand loving behavior. Fortunately, most preachers, it seems to me, save their souls in and through their commitment to the word. Their souls are grounded in the extravagant hope that what Jesus has promised will come to pass. Aware of the injustice and enmity within their own hearts and within the institutional Church, they preach justice and peace to themselves and to their Church. Conscious of their own failures to be loving men, they seek strength to love as Jesus loved. For these priests, preaching is both an act of humility and courage. The only way they dare name the grace of God active in the midst of their congregation is to rely on grace itself for the very act of naming grace.

Words that Wound

"Be careful with words," urges Elie Wiesel, "they're dangerous. Be wary of them. They beget either demons or angels."[18] For priests

---

[17]Bishop Carroll's letter, 1792 or 1794, is preserved in the Carmelite Monastery's archives in Baltimore.

[18]Elie Wiesel, *Legends of Our Time* (New York: Avon, 1968) 31.

familiar with the late Raymond Brown's work, Wiesel's warning is echoed in Brown's incisive comment, "In the Gospel the eagle soars above the earth, with talons bared for the fight. In the epistles we discover the eaglets tearing at each other for possession of the nest."[19] With the priests that have gone before them and with the priests that will come after, presbyters are ordained to speak words of liberation and healing. They tend the living word of God so that the word spoken on their lips may carry the passion and truth of the word made flesh. If they are faithful to their charge, they will be able to speak words that challenge and rebuke where behavior violates gospel tenets and values, but their words of fire and judgment will be understood as addressing the attitudes of heart and actions of sin rather than the enduring dignity of the human person.

As strange as it may seem, most words that wound are not the words spoken in the name of righteousness and justice, not the prophetic word the preacher and assembly need to hear, rather it is the misspoken pastoral word, thoughtless more often than mean-spirited or legalistic. It is the *clerical* word that enforces without listening carefully to parishioners' circumstances. It is the word that puts the image and policies of the institutional Church ahead of the pastoral well-being of the people of God. Sometimes it is a true word, a gospel word, spoken too soon or at the wrong time, giving the listener reason to believe that the priest knows only how to name sin and disgrace without searching for the movement of grace that often stirs in the most deplorable of situations.

Ecclesial words are at their worst when they become words of inquisition and accusation. The Inquisition, it can be argued, still exists though stripped of physical torture and the stake. It exists wherever an inquisitor takes the verbal formulations of the truths of our tradition and understands them as timeless absolutes whose meaning has once and for all been declared and confirmed. It exists whenever the essential truths of our faith are understood in such a manner that historical and contextual realities are dismissed out of hand. It exists when a cardinal's call to search out the common ground where polarized Catholics may meet for conversation is criticized by fellow cardinals as a possible threat to doctrinal purity. It exists when a cardinal's pastoral letter on the celebration of Eucharist is attacked as less than fully Catholic from the perspective of the accuser's self-declared orthodoxy. It exists wherever and whenever bishops and priests and

---

[19] As quoted in Kathleen Norris, *Amazing Grace* (New York: Riverhead Books, 1998) 219.

other members of the faithful speak words, even words of faith, out of fear rather than out of hope and love. These words, these holy words, wound rather than unite.

Tenders of the Imagination

Preaching a sermon entitled, "Is There Any Word from the Lord?" Paul Tillich acknowledged:

> Many of those who reject the Word of God reject it because the way we say it is utterly meaningless to them. They know the dimension of the eternal but they cannot accept our names for it. If we cling to their words, we may doubt whether they have received a word from the Lord. If we meet them as persons, we know they have.[20]

Tending to the word, the priest discovers, includes tending to the power and depth of his own imagination. The priest who takes preaching seriously takes his imagination seriously; he nourishes it with poetry and novels, with theater and film. He comes to understand that his imagination needs its own solitude, space, and time to interpret afresh the biblical symbols and the Christian message in such a way that they speak to questions and confusion, the blessings and tragedies that make up the human condition of his parishioners.[21]

When he thus respects his imagination, he finds that the core image of his homily often *comes* to him from his own depths. Those who hear his homily know without question that he is preaching from his head, heart, and imagination. They sense that the spirit of God is speaking through him. The words of his homily have been tended in the depth of his soul where they take their life from *the* word of God.

[20]Paul Tillich, "Is There Any Word from the Lord?" in *The New Being* (New York: Charles Scribner's Sons, 1955) 48.

[21]See Mary Catherine Hilkert, *Naming Grace*, chapter 1, "The Dialectical Imagination: The Power of the Word," 19–29.

Part III
Concerns

7

Considering Orientation

In the end, it is the reality of personal
relationships that saves everything.

—Thomas Merton

To love another, whether of the same sex or a different sex
is to have entered the area of the richest human experience.

—Cardinal Basil Hume

A few years ago I attended a West Coast meeting of seminary
rectors and deans. Sipping coffee before our first formal session, a
number of us alluded to the phenomenon of growing numbers of
homosexual seminarians. One of the rectors described a recent conversation that each of us acknowledged as both troubling and telling.
While in flight to the conference, he and another priest were review-
ing the agenda and the list of speakers invited to the meeting. A man
sitting in the window seat next to them overheard enough fragments
of their conversation to ask, "Are you two priests?" When told that,
yes, they were, he asked without hesitation, "Does that mean you're
gay?" Startled at the question, one of the priests inquired what led
him to make such an assumption. "Nothing in particular," he answered, "just impressions that took form in recent years."

I confess to a certain anxiety as I begin this reflection on homosexuality and the priesthood. Whatever is said about such a sensitive
and complex issue is open to misunderstanding and seeming insensitivity. Some will deny the reality that many observers see as changing
the face of the priesthood—that the percentage of homosexual priests
and seminarians is significantly higher than it is in society at large.
Others will see any attention given to the phenomenon as a symptom
of the homophobia that is characteristic of individuals with less than

97

open minds. Still others will wonder what difference sexual orientation makes in the celibate lives of priests. Regardless of the risks, the issue, I believe, deserves attention.

For more than a decade, now, voices have been heard expressing concern about the growing numbers of gay priests and seminarians.[1] Their call for serious reflection and candid discussion of the issue has largely gone unheeded. Attempts have been made, nonetheless, to address the issue administratively. In 1985, Cardinal Silvio Oddi, then head of the Congregation for the Clergy, said, "Candidates for the priesthood must be wisely culled, with particular attention paid to character weaknesses occasioned by the unnatural tendencies common in contemporary society."[2] Although Oddi did not explicitly mention homosexually oriented candidates, the meaning of his remarks is evident.

Earlier in 1985, the National Conference of Diocesan Vocation Directors published *Assessment of Applicants for Priesthood,* carefully addressing the issue:

> Is the applicant's sexual orientation public knowledge? If so, how will this affect his ministry? If not, does the applicant live with anxiety that it might become public? Does the applicant feel it should make no difference? Is this realistic in the setting of the diocese?[3]

Clearly, the issue is real.

The Estimates

Vicars of priests and seminary administrators who have been around awhile speak among themselves of the disproportionate number of gay men that populate our seminaries and presbyterates. They know that a proportionate number of gay priests and seminarians would fall between 5 and 10 percent. The extent of the estimated disproportion, naturally enough, will vary depending on general perceptions, personal experiences, and the frequency of first-hand encounters with self-acknowledged gay priests.

[1]See Richard P. McBrien, "Homosexuality and the Priesthood: Questions We Can't Keep in the Closet," *Commonweal* (June 19, 1987) 380–83, and Andrew Greeley, "Bishops Paralyzed Over Heavily Gay Priesthood," *National Catholic Reporter*, November 10, 1989, 13–14.

[2]Silvio Oddi, "You Are All and Nothing, O Priest," *National Catholic Register* (December 1, 1985) 5.

[3]P. Magnano, E. Schau, and S. Tokarski, *Assessment of Applicants for Priesthood* (Chicago: National Conference of Diocesan Vocation Directors, 1985) 32.

The general perceptions, in turn, are often shaped by various studies and surveys which attempt to measure the percentage of priests who are gay. An NBC report on celibacy and the clergy found that "anywhere from 23 percent to 58 percent" of the Catholic clergy have a homosexual orientation.[4] Other studies find that approximately half of American priests and seminarians are homosexually oriented. Sociologist James G. Wolf in his book *Gay Priests* concluded that 48.5 percent of priests and 55.1 percent of seminarians were gay.[5] The percentage appears to be highest among priests under forty years of age.[6] Moreover, the percentage of gay men among religious congregations of priests is believed to be even higher.[7] Beyond these estimates, of course, are priests who remain confused about their orientation and men who have so successfully denied their orientation, that in spite of predominantly same-sex erotic fantasies, they insist that they are heterosexual.

The Significance

So what, it may be asked, if the Catholic Church is developing a heavily homosexual priesthood? Few would deny that throughout the Church's history many priests, bishops, popes, and saints were homosexual in orientation. Aware that holiness of life and goodness of heart transcend orientation, that charisms for ministry and preaching are bestowed on God's people as God freely disposes, seminary admission committees tend to focus on the applicant's overall suitability for priestly service.

As a matter of practice, if not policy, many dioceses and religious congregations are open to ordaining gay men if they demonstrate a commitment to celibate living. They tend to be men who are nurturing,

---

[4]Timothy Unsworth, *The Last Priests in America* (New York: Crossroad, 1991) 248.

[5]See James G. Wolf, ed., *Gay Priests* (San Francisco: Harper and Row, 1989) 59–60. Wolf offers a word of caution, however, about his findings:

> It must be emphasized that these estimates are based solely on the impressions of the gay priests in our sample. . . . Several reviewers of this report have offered suggestions that cast doubt on the legitimacy of these estimates; others' comments lend support (60–61).

See also Raymond Hedin, *Married to the Church* (Bloomington & Indianapolis: Indiana University Press, 1995) especially 125–73.

[6]Unsworth, *The Last Priests in America*, 248.

[7]I heard a religious order priest with long experience in both formation and leadership state publicly at a conference on AIDS and the mission of the Church that 80 percent of his large East Coast order was gay.

intelligent, talented, and sensitive—qualities especially suited to ministry. Often they excel as liturgists and homilists. Without question, gay priests minister creatively and effectively at every level of pastoral leadership. The vast majority keep their orientation to themselves. Close friends and other gay priests know, but more often than not, parents and family are seldom informed. Perceptive parents and siblings may suspect, but in most cases let the matter rest.

Is homosexuality really a growing phenomenon in the priesthood or are we simply more aware of it than in past generations? I think both. Probably many of the gay priests of generations past had but the faintest notion of the nature of their sexuality. The closing decades of the twentieth century, however, witnessed a radical change in gay self-consciousness and awareness. While relatively few priests are "out" in the vernacular of the day, they are much more likely to be aware of and to acknowledge their gay orientation to a trusted circle of confidants. Nonetheless, it does appear that there are more gay priests at the turn of the century than there were at the middle of the last.

Approximately twenty thousand U.S. priests now have left the ministry, most in order to marry. Their absence, it can be argued, has dramatically changed the gay/straight ratio and contributed to the disproportionate number of priests with a homosexual orientation. Furthermore, the need gay priests have for friendship with other gay men, and their shaping of a social life largely comprised of other homosexually oriented men, has created a gay subculture in most of the larger U.S. dioceses. A similar subculture has occurred in many of our seminaries.[8] The growing numbers of gay priests and seminarians impact, of course, the priesthood's own self-awareness, even if on a subliminal level of consciousness. At the same time, it affects the laity's perception of their clergy. How would the laity respond should the priesthood become a heavily homosexual profession? Andrew Greeley answers:

> My impression is that most laypeople react sympathetically and compassionately and respectfully to a priest who might be gay so long as he is a good and hardworking priest, keeps his celibate promise and does not become part of the homosexual subculture. They would, I should note, also object to a heterosexual priest who became part of the singles

---

[8]Andrew Greeley believes that U.S. bishops, unclear on how to address the issue of expanding numbers of gay priests, have simply resorted to denial. Among the effects of this psychological defense mechanism is the toleration of lavender rectories and seminaries. "Bishops Paralyzed Over Heavily Gay Priesthood," *National Catholic Reporter* (November 10, 1989) 13–14.

bar scene. The lay reaction I describe would be quite independent of any conclusion they might have on the theoretical question of whether gay is "as good as" straight.

The laity, I suspect, would say it is one thing to accept a homosexual priest and quite another to accept a substantially homosexual clergy, many of whom are blatantly part of the gay subculture.[9]

Another question needs to be addressed. What impact does the gay subculture have on the straight priest and seminarian? My experience as a counselor and spiritual director to priests and seminarians suggests that straight men in a predominantly or significantly gay environment commonly experience chronic destabilization, a common symptom of which is self-doubt. The destabilization in question is similar to the unease that travelers encounter when moving about in countries whose language is unfamiliar to them. A certain awkwardness is common in these situations, sometimes accompanied by self-doubt and a loss of social confidence. It follows that a heterosexually oriented priest or seminarian gripped by a self-doubt that defies his best efforts to understand, wrestles with his own sense of self, his own identity. Their psychic confusion, understandably, has significant implications for both their spiritual vitality and emotional balance.

Homosexuality and the Seminary

Straight and gay seminarians, I believe, have different formational needs as they progress through their seminary years of preparation. Gay seminarians face specific challenges, of course, and their concerns, needs, and anxieties deserve the focused attention of formation faculties. The gay seminarian may live with considerable fear that his orientation may prove to be in itself an obstacle to advancing toward ordination. In some seminaries, the gay seminarians must deal with

[9]Ibid., 14. See also, Pastor Ignotus, "What Are We Advertising?" *The Tablet,* April 24, 1999:

> Equally disturbing is the tendency of bishops to overlook the fact that a disproportionate number of homosexuals are being recruited into our seminaries. I know of one seminary where, two years ago, 60 percent of the students identified themselves as "gay," 20 percent were confused about their sexual identity, and only 20 percent considered themselves to be heterosexual. I have no objection whatsoever to welcoming homosexuals into the priesthood. I know some excellent priests who are homosexual and that has never been a problem in their ministry. But there would be cause for concern if, in order to maintain the status quo, the Catholic priesthood were allowed to become primarily a "gay" option (553).

the implications of being a part of a minority. His spiritual and emotional needs deserve wise counsel and direction from his spiritual director and formation faculty. Under consideration here, however, are the formation issues facing the straight seminarian in the present seminary world.

Self-contained communities like seminaries with substantial gay populations present significant difficulties for the straight seminarian, often on an unconscious level. Unaware that his psyche senses a challenge to his own integration and identity—and therefore is standing on alert—he notices only a vague feeling of discomfort and a loss of psychic energy. The feeling that something is wrong may be pervasive and unrelenting. Even with healthy, close relationships with women and other straight men, the feeling that he is somehow out of sync, that he just doesn't seem to fit in with the others, may suggest to the seminarian that he is not called to the priesthood.[10]

A good deal of the seminarian's psychic energy, energy needed for study and prayer, is thus diverted into managing or coping with his inner turmoil. Only skilled spiritual directors and experienced faculty counselors are able to help the seminarian navigate these dangerous waters. Seminary formation faculties, unsure how to address the disproportionate number of gays and the formational implications of the situation, generally choose to approach the topic indirectly and, more often than not, on an individual basis through spiritual direction or counseling. When this is indeed the case, both the emotional climate of the seminary and the formation program itself suffer. Robert Nugent addressed the formation issue when he wrote,

> A "one size fits all" approach to celibacy formation without considering the unique differences among the candidates of age, life experiences, socio-cultural backgrounds and sexual orientation is no longer adequate given the changing ethos of Catholic life and ministry. A 22 year-old heterosexual, Hispanic, blue collar worker with a high school diploma, a 25 year-old, gay, university degreed, professional artist and a 52 year-

[10]See Annabel Miller, "This Endangered Species," *The Tablet* (April 24, 1999) 552–54. Miller observes:

> One criticism often made of the current seminary intake is that it is largely homosexual, and that the resulting ethos of the seminary causes the heterosexuals to leave. This was recognized in Fr. David Smith's paper for the bishops' conference in 1994. "With a higher proportion of homosexually inclined entrants," the document pointed out, "very often the heterosexual can feel in the wrong place. The image of the seminary is compromised" (553).

old, heterosexual, Polish widowed male with a bachelor's degree in accounting are shaped by their personal experiences and views of sexuality in ways that can not be adequately addressed by a highly idealized or over spiritualized celibacy formation program not in touch with the concepts, language and sexual realities of these diverse individuals.[11]

Compounding the challenge, of course, are seminary faculties which include a disproportionate number of homosexually oriented persons.

If disproportionate numbers of gay seminarians and priests present formational and pastoral dilemmas for the Church, a number of questions arise. What is a "proportionate" number of gay seminarians and priests? Should seminaries admit only a "proportionate" number of gay applicants? Should dioceses that accept homosexual candidates for the priesthood committed to the celibate life change their policy? How do seminary faculties show pastoral support to the seminarian who discovers his orientation well into his course of studies? How do seminary faculties address the gay subcultures that inevitably develop when significant numbers of the seminary community are gay?

These questions are important because the emergence of a subculture within a seminary or religious order based on sexual orientation is a serious challenge to the unity and integrity of the community, according to Timothy Radcliffe, Master of the Order of Preachers. Radcliffe writes,

> It can threaten the unity of the community; it can make it harder for the brethren to practice the chastity which we have vowed. It can put pressure on brethren to think of themselves in a way that is not central to their vocation as preachers of the Kingdom. . . .[12]

I believe rectors and formation faculties have yet to determine the kind of vocational support appropriate to the straight seminarian living in the midst of a gay subculture.

Should our seminaries become significantly gay, and many seasoned observers find them to be precisely that, the priesthood of the twenty-first century will likely be perceived as a predominantly gay profession. Some, we shall see, believe it has always been so.

---

[11]Robert Nugent, "Addressing Celibacy Issues with Gay and Lesbian Candidates," *Horizon* (Journal of the National Religious Vocation Conference) Fall 1998, 18.

[12]Timothy Radcliffe, O.P., *International Dominican Information*, no. 361, April 1998, special number, A Letter to the Order: "The Promise of Life," 96.

Throughout the Ages

While visiting the Greek Orthodox monasteries on Mt. Athos, the psychoanalyst and author Rollo May and his companions were struck

> by the feminine-like faces and bearing of many of the younger inhabitants (monks). . . . That might mean, we opined, that living in a country without women tends to make men more feminine. When we watched a monk walking down the street with his gown flowing, we would have sworn it was a woman. A man becomes a double sex, no doubt, when there are no women with whom to polarize his masculinity.[13]

Is May correct to propose that men living without women with whom they are able to polarize their masculinity will become feminine and, by inference, homosexual? Are men with feminine characteristics drawn to monasteries, seminaries, and other same sex life-styles or, once submerged in same sex communities, do they develop feminine characteristics and behaviors?

It appears that in most cases people do not choose their orientation. Rather they discover it. A biological disposition, some propose, intersects with crucial developmental dynamics resulting in a homosexual orientation.[14] Whether it's more *nature* or *nurture*—biological or psychological, political or a matter of preference—homosexual orientation as an expanding social phenomenon deserves attention and reflection. Now visible and vocal, gay men and lesbian women no longer allow the social and pastoral issues associated with orientation, especially formation issues, to be ignored. While the etiology and nature of homosexuality will continue to be explored in these early years of the twenty-first century, the history of homosexuality and the Church presents some interesting paradoxes.

When reminded of the distinction between sexual orientation and gay sexual behavior, many homosexuals protest that their orientation, in itself, does not demand a life of celibacy—precisely what they see the

---

[13]Rollo May, *My Quest for Beauty*, (Dallas: Saybrook, 1985). May continues:

> Or it might be due, on the other hand, to a desire on the part of the older monks for the company of young men who resembled the androgynous statues in the Athens Museum. I recalled the Greek ideal of figures who are both male and female shown in its statues, as we saw so beautifully in Hygeia (50).

[14]For a comprehensive review of the literature addressing the etiology of homosexuality, see John Boswell, *Christianity, Social Tolerance, and Homosexuality: Gay People in Western Europe from the Beginning of the Christian Era to the Fourteenth Century* (Chicago: The University of Chicago Press, 1980), especially n. 9, p. 9.

Church demanding of them. It's one thing, they assert, for bishops and priests to choose to live celibately, but church celibates should not seek to impose their celibate lifestyle on others based simply on orientation. The rejoinder that the Church calls all men and women who are not married, regardless of orientation, to sexual continence is simply ignored. Neither society nor the Church, they argue, recognize their covenant partnerships, and many dismiss out of hand the traditional teaching that there is to be no sexual expression throughout the entirety of their lives, even in cases of life-long monogamous commitment.

With notable exceptions, gay and lesbian activists have been critical, and even hostile to the Church's position on homosexuality. Feeling both misunderstood and abused, their animus toward the Church is one of their defining features at the turn of the century. So, it is of interest— if little consolation—that Yale historian John Boswell, in his award-winning *Christianity, Social Tolerance, and Homosexuality,* argued with meticulous scholarship and considerable wit that from the early middle ages, i.e., from about 500 to the end of the twelfth century, the Church provided homosexually oriented men and women with a safe haven during an especially chaotic and dangerous period.[15] That haven was religious life. Boswell reasons:

> Celibate religious life offered women escape from the consequences of marriage—for example, having to sleep with a husband and bear children—which might not only be unwanted but even life threatening. It afforded both genders a means of avoiding stereotypical gender roles. Women could exercise power in religious communities, among other women, without being subordinated to the male head of a household. Men could become part of a community of equals, all male, without the responsibilities of fatherhood or ruling a household; or they could exercise through the priesthood skills of nurturing and serving otherwise associated with women and considered shameful for men. Men could avoid obligations of warfare and devote themselves to study; women could become literate and learned, an opportunity rare for their sex outside religious communities after the decline of Rome.
>
> It is reasonable, under these circumstances, to believe that the priesthood and religious communities would have exercised a particular appeal for gay people. . . Indeed, lesbian and gay people would hardly have needed a spiritual motivation to join a same-sex community of equals.[16]

[15]Ibid.

[16]John Boswell, "Homosexuality and Religious Life: A Historical Approach," in *Homosexuality in the Priesthood and Religious Life,* ed. Jeannine Gramick (New York: Crossroad, 1989) 9.

Boswell's work provides a perspective that frames the current discussion about the disproportionate number of homosexuals among priests and seminarians: it has likely been this way for most of the Church's history. Homosexually oriented men and women of faith quite naturally find religious life and the celibate priesthood attractive. Often deeply spiritual with a desire to be of service to others and a natural inclination and aptitude for liturgical ritual, it is not surprising that Catholic gay men are attracted to the priesthood and religious life. Upon entering the seminary, there no longer is the need to explain to family and friends why they are not dating or married. The discipline of celibacy and being a spokesperson for a Church that insists upon celibate chastity for its clergy is a powerful help to holding in check sexual inclinations that are disturbing, even frightening, at least to some.

Novelist Julian Green, the first American elected to the *Academie Francaise,* spoke of being horrified to discover that his erotic interests focused on his male schoolmates. He described his homoerotic awakening as "desire mingled with terror."[17] Desire mingled with terror reinforced by the Church's warning of possible damnation should he act upon his desire becomes a strong motivating factor for a gay young Catholic to seriously consider a life as a priest or religious.

In the world of ecclesial celibate life, sexual orientation remains, on the surface, a mute issue. The relief can be enormous. The Trappist monk and writer Matthew Kelty supports Boswell's contention, writing:

> Since most men have a woman to love, whom is the gay man to love? God, surely, in the context of community and a noble, celibate service. This is the pattern of history, for then the sexual is absorbed in the loving communion with God and community.[18]

Both Boswell and Kelty paint a picture of religious life and celibate priesthood that is particularly suited to individuals who are homosexually oriented. From a theological perspective, their work raises a question one seldom hears: Is God more likely to bless gay men and women with the charism of celibacy than straight men and women? Or, from a slightly different angle, are gay people, by temperament and subtleties of spirit and soul, more likely than straights to be open to the charism of celibate, communal life? Kelty addresses this question when he observes, "It is my conviction that gays make superb celibates, the best

[17] *New York Times,* August 18, 1998, A 21.
[18] Matthew Kelty, "The Land I Love In," *Homosexuality in the Priesthood and Religious Life,* ed. Jeannine Gramick (New York: Crossroad, 1989) 148.

celibates, the more so in community. *I do not think the heterosexually oriented man should try to live celibacy*" (italics added).[19] From Kelty's perspective, the disproportionate number of gay priests, religious, and seminarians is anything but surprising. Rather it is quite understandable. Furthermore, the institutions of vowed religious life and celibate priesthood have provided life-styles and means of sanctification of immense importance to Catholic homosexuals—a point possibly overlooked by militant Catholic gays and lesbians frustrated by the Church's seeming intransigence on the disordered character of homosexual orientation and behavior.

The Priesthood as a Gay Profession

We will leave to the historians of culture and mores whether the priesthood and religious life have been disproportionately represented by homosexual men and women throughout the Church's history or whether this is a rather recent phenomenon. At issue at the beginning of the twenty-first century is the growing perception—one seldom contested by those who know the priesthood well—that the priesthood is or is becoming a gay profession. And to the point is the question: Does it matter? Does not the question reveal still another form of homophobia? Is it not another manifestation of discrimination and suspicion? Some would say the issue is best left alone, that we would all be better served not to notice the proverbial elephant in the room. Ignoring the phenomenon would certainly be easier than addressing it; yet closing our eyes to the situation only delays the time when circumstances will demand that it be given attention. In spite of the present glut of empirical studies and investigations, human sexuality, so intimately wedded to the life of the soul, still surpasses our full understanding and comprehension. And so, we waver. Nonetheless, it is right that we press on. Pastoral and formational concerns require that we do so.

The following questions, I believe, are fundamental: what are the pastoral implications for the Church at large should it fail to address the issue of homosexuality and the priesthood? What impact will

---

[19]Ibid. Kelty explains:

> It is too risky, for there seems small hope that the feminine of such a male will emerge in a culture such as ours, in which, until lately to a degree, men do not know how to relate to one another warmly and affectionately. They build poor communities, poor brotherhoods, cold and lacking in love. More integrated men can relate to one another warmly, heartily, without affection or fear. They can build beautiful communities and over the centuries have done so.

addressing the issue have on the large numbers of homosexual priests and religious who minister in fidelity to the Gospel? Still other questions come to mind. Over a decade ago, Richard McBrien raised a number of them in his essay "Homosexuality and the Priesthood: Questions We Can't Keep Out of the Closet."

> How many priests and seminarians are gay? How many of those are active homosexuals? What difference, if any, does the sexual orientation of a priest have on his pastoral ministry? Does it affect the gay priest's ministerial relations with heterosexual males, with women, with families, and their children? How does his homosexuality affect his relationship with heterosexual priests? Does the nature of these various relationships differ if the gay priest is sexually inactive rather than sexually active? What impact does the presence of a large number of gay seminarians have on the spiritual tone and moral atmosphere of our seminarians? Do gay seminarians inevitably create a gay culture in seminaries? To what extent are seminary faculty members a part of this culture? Are heterosexual seminarians "turned off" by the existence of such a culture? How many heterosexual seminarians have decided to leave the seminary and abandon their interest in a presbyteral vocation because of the presence of significant numbers of gays in seminaries and among the local clergy?[20]

The issue appears to be one of the major factors changing the face of the priesthood. It deserves compassionate and respectful attention.

Impact on vocations: It is now commonplace in Catholic circles to acknowledge that encouragement from mothers and parish priests are the two major factors that prompt a young man to consider the priesthood and apply for admission to a seminary. Gay priests who find themselves fulfilled and happy in the priesthood are likely, it would seem, to actively encourage the devout and eligible men of their parish to consider the priesthood. Since many, if not most, gay men are usually able to identify other gay men without any explicit acknowledgment of their orientation and are often more comfortable in the presence of gay men than straight men, it is likely that gay priests will be encouraging, consciously or unconsciously, more homosexually oriented men than straight men to consider a vocation to the priesthood. Conversely, homosexually oriented men considering a priestly vocation will be especially drawn to a parish priest who happens to be gay. Over the years there is no question but that gay priests have actively recruited and encouraged heterosexual men to consider life as priest. Still, the likelihood exists that like will be drawn to like.

[20]McBrien, "Homosexuality and the Priesthood," 380–83.

Perceptive mothers may sense that something is different about the pastor or associate of their parish who happens to be gay. Often they are not able to give a name to what their intuition seems to be telling them. They may indeed like and respect the priest, but find they are not comfortable in encouraging their son to consider the priesthood. Their hunch about their parish priest seems to be reinforced as they meet certain other priests in the course of their lives. Without necessarily speaking to another or even acknowledging their apprehension to themselves, they wonder if their son, whom they believe to be heterosexual in orientation, will be happy in a profession that appears to be populated by a significant number of gay men. Catholic fathers are no less likely to sense the presence of a considerable number of gay men among the priests he encounters during his school years and into his adult, married life. If not gay himself, he may share the same qualms that Catholic mothers experience.

The straight priest and seminarian: Inevitably, gay men form gay circles of friends and associates. While not necessarily exclusive by intention, these gay subgroups exercise an influence upon the straight men who find themselves either working with or living in close proximity to homosexual men. I proposed earlier that straight men in environments populated by significant numbers of gays experience a sense of destabilization. They wrestle with a certain self-doubt, a feeling that they don't fit in. On both psychic and spiritual levels, they are not "at home." Seminary faculties, in particular, need to pay attention to this phenomenon.

Out of the Clerical Closet

The last decades of the twentieth century witnessed the formation of informal and discreet networks of gay priests in most dioceses from coast to coast. Among themselves, it is clear, gay priests are comfortable with other gay priests knowing their orientation. Writing about religious life and homosexuality, Donald Goergen, O.P., argues that

> religious communities do not benefit from closeted homosexuality. I do not mean that men need to be public about their sexuality, a notion that seems to be an odd bane of our period of history. By closeted homosexuals I mean men who are closeted as regards their own selves. That is, they are significantly out of contact with their sexuality and thus unable to accept the degree or kind of homosexuality present in them; as a result, they are men who live in denial and fear and self-hatred. For homosexual men to live in religious communities, they need to be

comfortable enough to be unafraid of their homosexuality, and they certainly need to be able to acknowledge who they are to trusted friends.[21]

In addition to friendship and celibate intimacy, gay priests who share their identity with trusted friends have found support and understanding in a culture still grappling with the nature and significance of homosexuality amidst the unsettling demands of a vociferous gay rights movement. Some of these gay networks or subcultures are using the priesthood as cover for their sexual acting out, believing that their only responsibility to the Church is a certain discretion. Others are simply following the social instinct to find company with like individuals.

As gay priests come out among themselves (there is at least one Midwest congregation of religious men that I know of which holds a gay caucus when their members meet in assembly), religious and diocesan leadership need to distinguish between the celibate, both straight or gay, who is struggling and sometimes failing to be chaste and the priest or religious who coolly exploits the priesthood or the congregation for his own destructive purposes.

The priesthood's crisis of soul, and by extension, the Church's crisis of soul, is in part a crisis of orientation. Sooner or later the issue will be faced more forthrightly than it has in the closing decades of the twentieth century. The longer the delay, the greater the harm to the priesthood and to the Church.

[21]Donald Georgen, "Calling Forth a Healthy Chaste Life," *Review for Religious* (May–June 1998) vol. 57, no. 3, 268. See also William McDonough, "Acknowledging the Gift of Gay Priestly Celibacy," *Review for Religious*, vol. 55, no. 3 (May–June 1996) 283–96. McDonough writes:

> . . . I am not arguing here for public disclosure of sexual identity by gay clergy. I am looking for a twofold acknowledgment, one that is public and one that is personal. At the level of public discourse in the church, I am advocating the general acknowledgment that there are a significant number of homosexually oriented, celibate men in the priesthood. At the personal level I am suggesting something perhaps more costly to those directly affected: that homosexually oriented priests acknowledge at least to themselves the reality of their orientation (284).

8

Betraying Our Young

Of necessity, the party man
becomes a liar.

—Friedrich Nietzsche

Now I am a priest, with a boundless capacity for thwarting
good, and for turning wine into water.

—Pater Ignotus

In the 1940s, largely due to the critical and box-office success of
Going My Way and *The Bells of St. Mary's,* the Catholic priest, ideal-
ized in the gentle strength and beguiling charm of Bing Crosby's Fr.
Chuck O'Malley, captured the imagination of Catholics and non-
Catholics alike.[1] At a time when Catholics were still regarded with
considerable suspicion and hostility, an idealized and romanticized
Catholic subculture, personified in the charm of Father O'Malley, fascinated the U.S. movie-goer. Even to this day for Catholics over age
fifty, it is difficult to exaggerate Father O'Malley's hold on the
Catholic imagination's image of the ideal priest. How things have
changed.

Few, at that time, anticipated the collapse of the idealized, almost
heroic, image of the Catholic priest in film, television, and in the
imaginations of most Americans. The popular television series
M*A*S*H* portrayed Fr. Francis Mulcahy, the Catholic chaplain, as a
rather silly, simple, though good-hearted man. Priests now tend to be

[1]In 1944, *Going My Way* won six Oscars including: the award for best picture; Bing Crosby for best actor; Barry Fitzgerald for best supporting actor; and
Leo McCarey for the best original story and screen play.

portrayed as mostly soft men who are treated with condescending and patronizing fluff ("That a boy, Father"), or caricaturized as stiff, ecclesiastical sycophants obsessed more with what is forbidden than with what gives life and joy to the human heart.

The 1994 film *The Priest* portrayed a number of highly conflicted and deeply disturbed priests and their bishop coping sadly, even pathetically, with issues of human sexuality, authority, and power. The film effectively captured the shadow side of the priesthood, the side too often denied or sanitized by the official Church. But its unrelenting grimness overshadowed the graced humanity and goodness of priests in general. This failure allowed its many critics to dismiss the film, thereby missing a valuable artistic venue for examining and dealing with the darker side of the priesthood.

Still, nothing contributed more powerfully to the vastly different place in which priests are now held in both the Catholic and non-Catholic imaginations than the scandal of clergy misconduct with minors that surfaced in the mid 1980s. The tragedy's full impact on the Church and on the priesthood in particular remains to be weighed in the years and decades ahead. Some argue that there is nothing comparable to it in modern times. Without question, it has seared its victims, leaving them wounded and disillusioned. Families, especially the victim's parents, feel naïve for welcoming the offending priest into the heart of their home, without the slightest suspicion or mistrust. Soon the parents' "how could we have been so stupid?" question which followed their shock and disbelief evolves into anger and rage. Anger at the priest and, often enough, rage at diocesan leadership for its handling of the abuse. Recent years have seen the scandal spread to include bishops and other high-ranking prelates.

This eruption of criminality and immorality in the behaviors of priests and bishops has produced a number of books and essays addressing the scope of the crisis and the manner in which church authorities responded to it. Among the more notable books are Jason Berry's *Lead Us Not Into Temptation: Catholic Priests and the Sexual Abuse of Children*, A. W. Richard Sipe's *A Secret World: Sexuality and the Search for Celibacy*, and his *Sex, Priests, and Power: Anatomy of a Crisis*, and Stephen J. Rossetti's *A Tragic Grace: The Catholic Church and Child Sexual Abuse* and also by Rossetti, *Slayer of the Soul*.[2] These

---

[2]See Jason Berry, *Lead Us Not Into Temptation* (New York: Doubleday, 1992); A. W. Richard Sipe, *A Secret World* (New York: Brunner/Mazel, 1990), and *Sex, Priests, and Power* (New York: Brunner/Mazel, 1995); Stephen J. Rossetti, *A Tragic Grace* (Collegeville: The Liturgical Press, 1996), and *Slayer of the Soul* (Mystic, Conn.: Twenty-Third Publications, 1990); and Philip Jenkins, *Pedophiles*

books as well as many of the articles on the same subject have addressed the nature and scope of the problem and, in a few cases, uncover the meaning and significance of clergy misconduct with minors.[3] They remain important sources for anyone with the stomach to look deeply into the morass of this sorry situation which has caused so much pain to so many people and affected the morale and spirit of virtually every priest alive. What I offer here in this chapter is simply my reflections drawn from a half dozen years as vicar for clergy and religious in one of the larger U.S. dioceses—years that coincided with the height of the scandal.

As vicar, I met annually with chancellors and vicars from across the United States and discovered that the scandal took on similar characteristics in each of our dioceses relating to patterns of seduction, the scope of the problem, and responses from the community and the Church. The dioceses I became familiar with generally made serious efforts to bring about healing for the victims and their families and treatment for the priest-offenders. Underneath the scrambling efforts of bishops and vicars to respond effectively and pastorally to the crisis, questions about the meaning and implications of the violating behaviors were studiously avoided. We became absorbed with the task at hand: how to handle the present crisis, *this crisis.* I recall no thoughtful discussion about the causes of the problem, its meaning or implications. Attempts to do so were often met with a certain suspicion

---

and Priests (New York: Oxford University Press, 1996). Jenkins argues after a thorough and exhausting review of clergy sexual abuse cases that were reported by the media "that clergy sex abuse is far less widespread than the headlines suggest" (from dust jacket). In addition to the media, Jenkins points to liberal and traditionalist "dissidents" who seized upon the issue to further their own agenda for the exaggerations and misreadings that he sets out to correct.

[3] See Canice Connors, "Priests and Pedophilia: A Silence That Needs Breaking?" *America* (May 9, 1992) 400–01; John Allan Loftus, "Question of Disillusionment: Sexual Abuse Among the Clergy," *America* (December 1, 1990) 426–29; Jim Castelli, "Abuse of Faith: How to Understand the Crime of Priestly Pedophilia," *U.S. Catholic* (September 1993) 6–15; Peter Steinfels, "Needed: A Firm Purpose of Amendment," *Commonweal* (March 12, 1993) 16–18; Paul Wilkes, "Priests Who Prey," *New York Times* (May 6, 1993) A 21; Eugene Kennedy, "The See-no-problem, Hear-no-problem, Speak-no-problem Problem," *National Catholic Reporter* (March 19, 1993) 5; William Buckley, "The Church's Newest Cross," *National Review* (April 26, 1993) 63; Paul E. Dinter, "Celibacy and Its Discontents," *New York Times* (May 6, 1993) A 21; Andrew Greeley, "A View from the Priesthood," *Newsweek* (August 16, 1993) 45, and "How Serious Is the Problem of Sexual Abuse by Clergy?" *America* (March 20–27, 1993) 6–10; Donald Cozzens, "Pedophilia and the Priesthood," *The Plain Dealer* (September 4, 1987) B 9.

that a particular agenda was at work. Dioceses, to their credit, did move beyond anxious efforts to respond to individual cases by drafting policies to ensure pastorally sensitive and legally sound inquiries and responses to allegations of clergy sexual misconduct. Yet, to my knowledge, no serious investigation has been launched into the origin of clergy misconduct with minors; no review of the clergy's higher incident rates.[4]

No one, of course, wanted to exaggerate the problem. Yet diocesan officials would be naïve to think that there are not numerous incidents of clergy misconduct with minors that have not come to their attention. No doubt a certain institutional denial is understandable. Instead of wrestling with admittedly difficult questions that may in the end escape even partial, tentative answers, bishops and diocesan spokespersons emphasized that the problem of clergy misconduct with minors was simply a slice of a broader social problem; they pointed out that most pedophiles were married men; and, predictably, that there is a higher incident rate for this kind of abuse among teachers, coaches, scout leaders, and other professionals who work with youngsters.

It became clear that no other issue was recasting the face of the priesthood with more slashing and broad strokes than the sexual misconduct of priests and bishops with minors. Story after story in both the print and electronic media generated waves of numbness and bewilderment in priests and Catholics in general. As the numbness of shock subsided, priests began to feel a kind of guilt. Some, it appeared, had failed to heed the age-old axiom "see what you see, hear what you hear." Had they missed signs, even persistent signs, that something was wrong? John Dreese, writing in *Commonweal,* put it this way:

> In one of my early assignments the senior associate was known to be a friend of the boys in the parish. He always had a couple of junior high school boys with him. One evening, when I entered the rectory, this priest was in the living room with two of them. He told me that they

[4]See Rossetti, *A Tragic Grace.* Rossetti, president of The Saint Luke Institute, a psychiatric treatment center for clergy and religious that has treated a large number of the priests who have crossed boundaries with minors, writes:

> Despite the lack of empirical statistics, my clinical experience suggests that approximately 2 to 7 percent of Catholic clergy are sexually involved with minors at some point in their priestly lives. . . . Many people ask how this figure of 2 to 7 percent compares with the general population of males. The answer is, "We do not know" (117).

What Rossetti's figures do not include and cannot include, of course, are the estimates of priests who have not acted out yet find themselves sexually interested in minors.

were busy and asked me to leave the living room. I left, but I thought it strange that he would order me out to make room for the two teen-agers. This same priest was considered a guru to teen-age boys in other parishes. Years later he was convicted of sexually abusing boys and served a prison sentence. What I suspected, but did not want to believe, had happened. Suspicion, however, is not proof. In today's climate I would confront the man. . . . I gave him the benefit of the doubt, and, as far as I know, so did everyone else.[5]

For most the guilt was short-lived. The problem, after all, had not yet sprung into the forefront of Catholic consciousness and the dysfunction spawning the misconduct was just beginning to surface. As the guilt subsided, priests noticed a growing suspicion on the part of parents with children in the parish school or teenagers active in youth programs. "Will there be other chaperones besides the associate pastor on the youth retreat?" the parish secretary is asked. Some priests remained angry with their colleagues who betrayed their fraternity:

Mixed with feelings of shame and embarrassment there is great anger. I am angry at the priest-pederasts and abusers. . . . If they knew what they were doing but could not control a compulsion to act out, then they were clearly sick. At this point they had two choices: to get professional help or to get out of the priesthood.[6]

Instead of anger, my own response to the scandal was more sadness; on those days when I drove from my office at the Catholic Center after meeting with either a victim of clergy abuse or the priest-abuser, the sadness was palpable. It was particularly acute when the accused priest acknowledged that the report was substantially accurate. In these cases there was no dispute about the allegation itself, but rather how the Church would respond to the victim, how the priest might attempt some reconciling behavior, how the Church would minister to the victim and abuser. And, if the abuse was reported in the media, how the Church would minister to the parish community.

On a few occasions, I was faced with the task of informing a congregation that their pastor or associate had been reported for misconduct with a minor or minors and that, following diocesan policy, he would be required to temporarily step down until an investigation could be undertaken and a psychological assessment could be completed. The pall of stunned silence that invariably came over the congregation

[5]John J. Dreese, "The Other Victims of Priest Pedophilia," *Commonweal* (April 22, 1994) 12.
[6]Ibid., 11–12.

(usually I spoke at the conclusion of Sunday Eucharist) and the look of shocked disbelief on the faces before me are logged firmly in my memory. I felt an even keener pain on those occasions when I visited the home of a young man or woman who fell victim to the sexual advances of a priest.

Most dioceses, I believe, tried to respond to allegations of clergy misconduct with honest pastoral concern for the alleged victim and, at the same time, with concern for the canonical and legal rights of the accused priest. Maintaining this two-fold responsibility proved challenging in many cases. If the complaint was deemed credible by diocesan staff, the accused priest was offended that an investigation was undertaken in light of his years of untarnished service. If the Church's pastoral response to the victim, no matter how appropriate, acknowledged that the accused priest was entitled to due process, the rejoinder from victim and family, at least from time to time, was anger and even outrage. Sometimes my contact with accuser and accused brought me to suspect that both would pass lie-detector tests had they agreed to the procedure. Most cases, however, were less ambiguous. Still, the responsibility of responding pastorally, responding as Church, was seldom easy.

The temptation to respond as a corporation, to put concern for diocesan assets and the Church's image before pastoral issues, was real. The tendency in some dioceses to respond as a corporation would be reinforced, of course, when extravagant sums of money were sought, especially through civil suits and in those cases where an allegation proved to be unsubstantiated. Serious mistakes, nonetheless, were made in numerous dioceses that compounded already disastrous situations. In recent years there has been a marked improvement in the institutional Church's response to allegations of clergy misconduct. The National Conference of Catholic Bishops, religious congregations, and local churches have addressed the issue with a forthrightness and candor not seen a decade ago. Particularly courageous has been the unprecedented action taken by the Irish Christian Brothers in March 1998. After serious and careful deliberations as a religious congregation, the Christian Brothers made the following public apology. It ran in national newspapers throughout the Republic and in Northern Ireland. Quoted in its entirety on page 117 is the advertisement published on March 30, 1998, in *The Irish Times*.

The Order's apology and honest steps to address any wrongdoing on the part of its brothers is a significant turn. Whether it will influence other religious congregations and diocesan policies remains to be seen. Stephen Rossetti reinforces the power of apology as the first step in the Church's response to clergy misconduct:

**Message from the
Irish Christian Brothers**

Over the past number of years we have received from former pupils
serious complaints of ill-treatment and abuse by some Christian
Brothers in schools and residential centres.

We, the Christian Brothers in Ireland, wish to express our deep
regret to anyone who suffered ill-treatment while in our care.

And we say to you who have experienced physical or sexual abuse
by a Christian Brother, and to you who complained
of abuse and were not listened to, we are deeply sorry.

We want to do more than say that we are sorry. As an initial step, we
have already put in place a range of services to offer a practical
response. Further services will be provided as needs become clearer.

For independent and confidential help and advice phone:

Freephone *Faoiseamh* Helpline

1 800 33 1234   Republic
0 800 97 3272   Northern Ireland

(Monday to Saturday 10.00 a.m. to 10.00 p.m.)

or contact us directly:

The Irish Christian Brothers	The Irish Christian Brothers
P.O. Box 6245	Freepost
Freepost	Dept. IE 8018
Dublin 7	P.O. Box 788
	Belfast
	BT1 1XX

I remember being at a parish where a pastor had been charged with
child sexual abuse and was removed. The parishioners were devastated
and came in large numbers to a town meeting with the diocesan chancellor. As the meeting progressed, the chancellor became more defensive and the people became angrier. Voices got louder and more shrill.
Finally, just when it seemed like the meeting would explode, the chancellor said, "I am sorry. This is a terrible thing and it should never have
happened." Immediately, the atmosphere in the room changed. The
tension level dropped. Voices quieted. The victims and their families
heard what they needed.[7]

[7]Rossetti, *A Tragic Grace*, 107.

When the Archdiocese of Chicago announced its comprehensive and pace-setting policy on clergy sexual misconduct with minors, some diocesan attorneys expressed concern. It was feared that apologies, especially public apologies, and a non-adversarial openness to the concerns of those making reports of clergy misconduct would open the gates to litigation thereby threatening a diocese's solvency and financial reserves. The $118,000,000 judgment against the Diocese of Dallas, it was reasoned, could happen anywhere.[8] Still, the position taken by the Archdiocese of Chicago and the courageous and humble action of the Irish Christian Brothers deserve emulation. I'm convinced that responding to the crisis as Church, with pastoral concern for the victims and with keen alertness to the possibility of false or unsubstantiated allegations, is the most responsible and effective way to exercise stewardship over the Church's resources.

Another Aspect of the Crisis

A number of commentators believe that the debacle of clergy sexual misconduct with minors is revealing more than the human frailty and pathology of a relatively small number of priests and bishops. They propose that the crisis is pointing to a cancer in the very systemic structure of the priesthood and hierarchy.[9] *Systemic structure* as used here includes those ecclesial patterns of communication, operation, and discipline that both define the lives of the ordained and facilitate their exercise of authority and power.[10] It includes an almost infinite number of cues, signs, and symbols of identity and power that constitute the present clerical and hierarchical culture and world. Is it not possible, they reason, that the problem of priests' sexual contact with minors, while tragic in its own right, is more than an overflow of a societal problem into the ranks of priests and bishops? Priests are human, the defense goes, some will have a problem with alcohol, others with money and possessions, and some will be sexually attracted to

[8]See Pamela Schaeffer, "Sex Victims Win Big against Dallas, Priest," *National Catholic Reporter*, August 1, 1997, 3–4.

[9]See Thomas C. Fox, *Sexuality and Catholicism* (New York: George Braziller, 1995), and A. W. Richard Sipe, *Sex, Priests, and Power* (New York: Brunner/Mazel, 1995), especially chapter 5, "System: Function/Dysfunction," 83–111.

[10]See Peter M. Senge, *The Fifth Discipline* (New York: Currency and Doubleday, 1990). Senge insists that "it is very important to understand that when we use the term 'systemic structure' we do not just mean structure outside the individual. The nature of structure in human systems is subtle because *we* are part of the structure" (44).

children and teenagers. It's a human, moral problem, not a systemic problem.

Priests, according to this line of thinking, are no more drawn to pedophilia and ephebophilia (the recurrent, intense, sexual interest in post-pubescent youths, generally between the ages of 13 or 14 and 17) than other professionals who work with children and young people. The explanation offers consolation and a useful rationalization for those who find the present clerical system compatible with their personal needs, with those who feel the rightness of the system as the clear gift of the Spirit, and with those who feel compelled, out of a sense of ecclesial loyalty, to uphold the current system without critical reflection.

Defenders of the present system see probes of this kind as subversive of the priesthood itself and as thinly disguised attempts to change the present practice and discipline of the Church, especially the discipline of obligatory celibacy for the Latin rite.[11] An open, mature Church, one would think, would welcome reflection and discussion on its policies, practices, and disciplines. These are not matters of revelation or doctrine. Furthermore, to insist that there is simply no correlation between mandatory celibacy and the present crisis over clergy misconduct with minors looks like bureaucratic bullying as long as the Vatican remains opposed to even discussion concerning the systems undergirding the priestly lifestyle. And it is clear that the Vatican does not want even some disciplinary practices, including celibacy, to be discussed and looks upon bishops and priests who call for discussion as dissidents.[12] Bishops will privately acknowledge that Pope John Paul II explicitly forbade them to discuss "contraception, abortion, homosexuality, masturbation, a married priesthood or women's ordination to the priesthood other than to defend the Church's official teaching."[13]

Those who mention in conversation that they do not see mandatory celibacy as inherent to the priesthood are suspected of disloyalty. A sad effect of this hard-line is the muting of those voices that believe we have nothing to fear in discussing or examining the sexual/celibate/power systems that presently define the priesthood and episcopacy. Such discussions may lead to insights into the negative aspects of the clerical system that may be creating an atmosphere or a set of circumstances that in turn foster the kinds of behaviors at the core of the present crisis.

---

[11]See Jenkins, *Pedophiles and Priests.*
[12]Fox, *Sexuality and Catholicism*, 166.
[13]Sipe, *Sex, Priests, and Power*, 44.

It is generally acknowledged in seminary formation circles that parish ministry and leadership require significantly high levels of emotional and spiritual maturity. Parish ministry, then, is especially dangerous for celibate priests who are affectively underdeveloped. What happens to the immature priest who is drawn to the priesthood for the very reasons that put people at risk for compensatory acting out with individuals who are not of their age—fear of intimacy and resistance to healthy risk taking? We need to ask if the clerical system itself may be setting the table for misconduct with minors. In other words, do we have a system that spiritually and emotionally immature individuals find inviting? The answer may be a resounding no, but our unwillingness to look beyond and beneath the behaviors involved in clergy abuse appears indefensible.

Stephen Rossetti has identified a number of red flags for child sexual abuse.[14] Among them is the absence of healthy and intimate relationships with peers. The opportunity afforded clergy to relate formally with individuals and to keep a certain clerical distance from parishioners and other adults may suit the immature priest just fine.[15] We need to determine if the systemic structure of the clerical culture and world is unwittingly attracting individuals at risk for misconduct with minors, and we need to determine if the priesthood's systemic structure itself encourages and fosters healthy spiritual and emotional growth in its members. This will require far more than clergy workshops on boundary violations—important as these workshops are. I fear, however, that the kind of study and analysis the present crisis calls for will prove too threatening in the present climate of suspicion and mistrust.

Impressions of a Vicar

Not surprisingly, as I listened to the reports of victims of sexual abuse, I was struck by the pain I heard in their voices, and behind the pain, courage. No small amount of courage was required to call the diocese, to meet with a diocesan official at the Catholic Center or chancery, and to explain the nature and pattern of the priest's misconduct. And behind the courage, fear—fear that no one would believe them; that it would come down to their word against the priest's

[14]See Stephen Rossetti, "Some Red Flags for Child Sexual Abuse," *Human Development,* vol. 15, no. 4 (1994) 5–11.

[15]Ibid., 6–10. Other red flags include confusion about sexual orientation; childish interests and behavior; extremes in developmental sexual experiences; personal history of childhood sexual abuse and/or deviant sexual experiences; an excessively passive, dependent, conforming personality.

word; fear that somehow they would be blamed for "allowing" the abuse to continue, sometimes for a number of years; fear that they would be deemed the enemy in the eyes of church authorities.

In most cases, somewhere in the mix of these emotions, was an understandable anger that was both righteous and ambiguous. It was righteous, because in the majority of reports where the allegation was grounded in actual abuse, a member of the Church suffered a profound injustice from one of the Church's official "promoters of justice." It was ambiguous, because the victim often, I sensed, wanted the priest to suffer as they had suffered. They wanted someone to pay for their loss of innocence. While rightful retribution is supported by the Gospel, vengeance is not. In some of the victims, especially after large pre-trial settlements and jury awards had been reported in the media, there was an urgent striving to "get my fair share."[16] Most victims I worked with simply wanted to be morally certain that the priest would not be allowed to harm others and that they would receive the therapy necessary for them to put their lives back together.

Because tending to the victims and their families was often enough emotionally draining, it's somewhat understandable that church authorities didn't have the energy to look beyond the urgent actions and important decisions associated with crisis management: responding pastorally to the parties involved, complying with local and state statutes, and making an all-out effort at understanding the truth of the situation. That failure, nevertheless, to look beyond the immediate problem of dealing with a particular case of clergy abuse to the underlying causes of the crisis may be as serious a mistake as the administrative bungling and pastoral insensitivity that was common in the early years of the scandal.

Furthermore, there are senior voices in leadership positions that fiercely insist that any soul searching of this nature is a kind of infidelity to the Church and the present discipline of the priesthood. For these voices, the scandal was simply another example of human frailty, the old "the flesh is weak" wisdom so supported by human history. Thus the Church turned from an all-out effort at understanding the larger network of forces that were supporting and contributing to the crisis, leaving any analysis of the ecclesial systems at work in the scandal to others.

So it is not surprising that in many corridors of the institutional Church a defensive posture took hold. Church spokespersons reminded the public that only a very small percentage of priests were implicated

---

[16]Conservative estimates place the amount paid to victims of clergy sexual abuse by the mid-1990s at half a billion dollars.

in the problem and that the problem was not limited to Catholic priests. Thus contextualized, it made sense to focus almost exclusively on the cases at hand. Some Catholic commentators began scapegoating: it was the media's fault and/or a manifestation of the still virulent anti-Catholic bias in American life. While the media seemed to take a certain relish in placing priest misconduct stories where they couldn't be missed, I felt it was a mistake to blame them for exacerbating the scandal. I often heard the remark that if a minister or rabbi had been accused of similar misconduct the story would have been buried deep in the paper or briefly noted on the television news reports. Yet from the reporters' and editors' perspective, the Church makes claims that are likely to appear smug and self-righteous to the secular professionals who make up a good portion of the media's ranks.

From an outsider's point of view Catholics claim to be the one true Church (most are not familiar with the council's decree on *Religious Freedom*) and believe that their priests have the power to change bread and wine into the body and blood of Jesus Christ. On top of that, the Church asserts that priests can forgive people's sins. This perspective, of course, reveals a serious lack of theological understanding of the ministry of the priest, the central role of the Holy Spirit, and the gathered assembly in the sacramental life of the Church. Yet from the media's vantagepoint, the asserted spiritual powers of the priest are staggering to the man or woman who does not share our faith. When someone with these asserted powers falls, it is *news!*

Of course, other quite human motives are likely at work whenever the media report Catholic clergy cases of sexual abuse with minors. Conceding, at times, the worst of these motives, it still remains a strategic mistake to insist the media is a major factor in the scandal under discussion.[17] Nor do I see some anti-Catholic conspiracy at work here. The climate has thawed considerably since Arthur M. Schlesinger's oft-quoted observation to John Tracy Ellis, "I regard the prejudice against your Church as the deepest bias in the history of the American people."[18] While the bias still holds in many quarters of the nation and the crisis is surely being exploited by those who look with suspicion and fear upon the Church, the root of the problem remains in our own history.

[17]For an argument supporting the opposite of my position, see Jenkins, *Pedophiles and Priests*, chapter 4: "The Media and the Crisis," 53–76.

[18]John Tracy Ellis, *American Catholicism*, 2nd ed., revised (Chicago: University of Chicago Press, 1969) 151.

What kind of men are these? During my years as vicar, I investigated dozens of reports of clergy sexual misconduct, spending a good part of many working days arranging for assessment and treatment for accused priests. In only a few cases did I suspect the priest sitting across from me possessed a heart of stone. The majority of these priests were effective enough pastors, and some were highly regarded for the skill and commitment that marked their service and leadership. No matter how effective they were as priests, no matter how good their "hearts" might be, they were men who had grievously wounded young people, often through patient patterns of seduction. Like their brother priests, they were wounded healers.

Unlike the great majority of their brother priests, they had betrayed the more vulnerable members of the Church in behaviors both criminal and immoral. They had betrayed a sacred trust. Without wanting to diminish the harm they had done, there seemed to be something amiss at the core of their personalities. For I sensed almost no guilt whatsoever for their seductions. The only regret I could identify was associated with being caught. For the most part, the men I worked with were more concerned about themselves and their futures than for their victims.[19] From my relatively brief work with them I came to regard them as focused sociopaths—little or no moral sense, no feelings of guilt and remorse for what they had done at least in *this area* of their lives. When it came to their misconduct with minors there was no evidence of conscience. I remember having to ask, "Are you sorry for the harm you did, for the suffering of the victim?" They answered, not surprisingly, "Yes"—but with little conviction. I don't remember one priest acknowledging any kind of moral torment for the behaviors that got him in trouble. The absence of remorse and concern for their victims continues to trouble me.

What is different about priest abusers? When vicars of priests met to learn from one another how we might better minister to the victims of clergy sexual misconduct, we discovered a factor that put priest offenders at variance with the general population of child abusers. As a group, abusers tend to be married men who prey on

---

[19]See Sean D. Sammon's forward to Stephen Rossetti, *Slayer of the Soul* (Mystic, Conn.: Twenty-Third Publications, 1990). Sammon notes that many child abusers are described as "me-first" individuals who find sexual relationships with children safer and less threatening than relationships with peers (vii–viii). In the same volume see Anonymous, "A Priest Child Abuser Speaks," 99–111. The author outlines his own abuse as a child and describes his experiences in prison. His story, indeed tragic and sad in its own right, did not allude even once to the harm he had inflicted on his victims nor did he express any concern for their welfare.

girls, although many pedophiles abuse both girls and boys. Our respective diocesan experience revealed that roughly 90 percent of priest abusers targeted teenage boys as their victims. Most priest abusers, we concluded, were not pedophiles in the strict sense of the term. They tended to be *ephebophiles,* adults whose sexual interest focused on post-pubescent teenagers, and in the case of the vast majority of priest offenders, on male teenagers. We found this factor to be a constant variable in the cases brought to our dioceses' attention. Relatively little attention has been paid to this phenomenon by church authorities. Perhaps it is feared that it will call attention to the disproportionate number of gay priests. While homosexually oriented people are no more likely to be drawn to misconduct with minors than straight people, our own experience was clear and, I believe, significant. Most priest offenders, we vicars agreed, acted out against teenage boys.

Is clergy misconduct with minors a recent phenomenon? It would seem not. A cursory review of early church documents suggests that clergy abuse of minors has been a concern from the first years of the Church's history. The *Didache,* the early-second-century commentary on the Gospels, sternly warns, "Thou shalt not seduce young boys."[20] Two centuries later, John Cassian (c. 365–c. 435), one of the early monastic giants of the West, admonished, "Let no one, especially when among young folk, remain alone with another even for a short time, or withdraw with him or take him by the hand."[21] Pope Julius III, who reigned from 1550 to 1555, created a scandal when he picked up a fifteen-year-old boy from the streets of Parma and named him a cardinal and Secretary of State.[22] The cardinal could not have been older than twenty when Julius III died in 1555. Our own age, it appears, is now ready to hear the voices of those who have been abused physically or sexually.

While the phenomenon may be as old as the priesthood itself, we still struggle to understand the scope of the problem. Most victims simply never come forward. William Reid claims that "careful studies have indicated . . . that child molesters commit an average of sixty offenses for every incident that comes to public attention."[23] Thomas

[20]M. Foucault, *Politics, Philosophy, Culture: Interviews and Other Writings 1977–1984,* ed. L. Kritzman (New York: Routledge, 1988) 232.

[21]Ibid., 233.

[22]Richard P. McBrien, *Lives of the Popes* (San Francisco: Harper, 1997) 283.

[23]William H. Reid, *The Psychiatric Times,* April 24, 1988, quoted in Sipe, *Sex, Priests, and Power: Anatomy of a Crisis,* 25.

Fox, at the other end of the estimates, reports that the "average pe-dophile priest abuses 285 victims."[24] By the mid 1990s it was esti-mated that some six hundred priests had been named in abuse cases and more than half a billion dollars had been paid in jury awards, settlements, and legal fees.[25]

Estimated costs of sexual abuse of minors by clergy do not include the church-absorbed expense of psychological and counseling treat-ment for victims and the priest predators. In the latter case, psychiatric treatment for priest pedophiles and ephebophiles, which often includes six months of care in psychiatric centers specializing in services to priests and religious, regularly reaches six figures for an individual priest. When these assessment and therapeutic expenses are included, the financial drain on the U.S. Church far exceeds the half billion estimate.

In recent years bishops and religious orders like the Irish Christian Brothers have made significant strides in responding pastorally to the clergy abuse crisis. Victims reporting abuse are far less likely to feel they are dealing with an impersonal corporate structure as they sit down with diocesan officials. This sea change in the Church's response should not be overlooked. What still needs urgent attention, however, are the systemic structures of clerical culture which appear to be im-portant variables in the etiology of the crisis. How much of the current crisis remains under the surface can only be guessed. What is certain, however, is the depth and darkness of the waters.

·

[24]Thomas C. Fox, "Sex and Power Issues Expand Clergy-Lay Rift," *National Catholic Reporter* (November 13, 1992) 17–19.
[25]Fox, *Sexuality and Catholicism*, 188ff.

Part IV
Realities

9

The Changing Face of the Priesthood

Love touches us spontaneously
and it makes us spontaneous.

—Bernard of Clairvaux

In humility is perfect freedom.

—Thomas Merton

A generation has now elapsed since the close of the council. For most priests ordained before or during the council, the great surprise of Pope John XXIII awakened a sense of anticipation and hope unprecedented during their lifetimes. Bishops, too, felt the excitement as they reclaimed their ancient identity as members of the college of bishops. The laity, awakened and stirred by the summons to active lives of holiness, stretched their sacramental imagination and took their rightful place in the ecclesial community. Now, it was understood, everyone was called to holiness, every baptized person called to service and ministry in accord with his or her own gifts and talents.

Clearly, a new identity buoyed up the Church and challenged it to bring the Gospel to the crossroads and networks of the global village. The priest's role in the pastoral and evangelizing mission of the Church remained central, but now somehow slightly out of focus. The post-conciliar Church called for a different way of being a priest, as we saw in Chapter 1, and the new way was only just beginning to be understood. And then the troubles, brewing one might argue from the intellectual dampening of the early twentieth century modernist controversy and the skewed approaches to spirituality flourishing in eighteenth- and nineteenth-century seminaries, began to erupt precisely at the moment when the priest was least sure of himself.

The post-conciliar years have tested the mettle of priests—crisis after crisis "shaking their foundations" and turning their lives inside out and upside down. They have looked inward in search of their core identity; wrestled with their conscience to maintain their integrity; haltingly acknowledged a need, linked to the very soul of their spirituality, for authentic, human intimacy. During these years they watched as almost half of their peers left active ministry, some clearly the best and the brightest. Deep wounds rented the fabric of the clerical image. Much of the privilege was gone. Most were pleased. A good deal of the trust and regard were gone. Most were saddened. They were saddened, too, that the promise of real dialogue with their bishops was never realized. When bishops did speak with their priests, they seemed to listen as wise teachers seeking only to answer the questions of their less experienced students and to communicate papal and curial directives.

During the 1970s and 1980s priests saw the polarization that surfaced during the council widen as curial officials struggled to hold on to their ground and differing ecclesiologies undercut the priesthood's common ground. After a while priests became accustomed to the lack of real dialogue. The hope and energy left most of their eyes. Many priests simply settled into making their lives "work" by pastoring to the best of their ability, by shrinking their world to the borders of their parishes. Large numbers resigned to pursue less conflicted life in the sacrament of marriage. Some priests simply went through the motions, husbanding their energies for comforts and pursuits that dulled their profound disappointment. A few became cynical and bitter. The rest, I believe, held to the conviction that eventually the confusion and angst would be soothed by the liberating breath of the Spirit.

Elsewhere I described this period following the council, especially the last two decades, as the priesthood's dark night.[1] The dark night, John of the Cross writes, draws us into periods of aridity and emptiness where even prayer becomes laborious and the soul is bereft of consolation. But the darkness of the priests' night permitted a deepening and purifying of their souls. For the ordeal of the dark night, ultimately, proved to be a blessing, a grace. In the collective dark night that engulfed priests these past two decades, they walked as men in a fog, unsure of their identity and mission. Reactionary conservatives traced the darkness' origin to the liberalizing, heady, pseudo-freedom they saw surfacing after the council; a freedom deeply mistrusted

---

[1]Donald B. Cozzens, "Priesthood Emerges From a Dark Night," *America,* vol. 180, no. 9 (March 20, 1999) 24.

because, in their eyes, it threatened to erode the transcendental splendor they associated with the Baroque period of Catholic culture.[2]

For the neo-conservative Catholic, any dark night the priest might be suffering was traced to the Church's infidelity to the pre-conciliar structures and practices that resonated with such surety and clarity amidst the social chaos and moral relativity of modernity. For other Catholics, however, and for most priests, I believe, the dark night was the work of the Spirit, leading priests through dark valleys only to bring them to a point where they could see new horizons. The darkness was necessary to bring about a conversion of mind and heart, to effect a new way of seeing and listening, an *aggiornamento*. In the midst of the dark night priests stood in a fire of transformation and conversion. Stripped of the cultural supports and roles that shaped their identity and mission, they were pressed to ask, as if for the first time, what it meant to be a priest; what it meant to be *one of the faithful* and their servant-leader; what it meant to be a tender of the word.

As they stood in the fire of purification, priests came to see afresh the unique importance of the priesthood and, at the same time, the holiness and dignity of the whole people of God. They were leaders of the people of God but also partners with them in building up the reign of God in history. As members of the church community, they co-labored with non-ordained pastoral ministers and with parishioners who enjoyed gifts of ministry and service. As the new horizon came into focus, priests became convinced of two truths in particular: the abiding presence of God guiding the Church's movement toward the new horizon and an equally inspired conviction that residual questions and issues long denied or minimized needed to be faced. A failure of nerve to look honestly at the wounds and failures of priests and bishops would, it was understood, lead to a different, unholy darkness.

There is little doubt in the minds of priests that the Church stands at a precarious point at the turn of the millennium. The honesty and courage required of the Church, especially of its episcopal and presbyteral leaders, is considerable. Turning from the challenge, the new horizon inspired by the Second Vatican Council will slip from view. Should we allow the new horizon to disappear, the very mission of the Church would be threatened. We turn now to consider some of the critical questions and issues that are changing the face of the priesthood and possibly the face of the Church.

[2]See Thomas F. O'Meara, "Leaving the Baroque: The Fallacy of Restoration in the Postconciliar Era," *America*, vol. 174, no. 3 (February 3, 1996) 10–14, 25–28.

The Vocation Crisis

For most readers there is little need to review the staggering drop in the number of candidates studying for the priesthood in the theologates of North America and western Europe (c. 80 percent), nor the roughly 40 percent decline in the number of priests in these same geographical regions during the last three decades of the twentieth century. Some, however, may be unaware of the small number of priests under age forty. In the Diocese of Cleveland, for example, there were 240 priests age forty and under in 1970. In 1999 there were only 35. Researchers predict that by the year 2005, only one in eight priests will be under age thirty-five with the average age of priests close to sixty. These dramatic declines are occurring at a time when the Catholic population is escalating, especially in the U.S. Twenty years ago there was approximately one priest for every 1,000 Catholics; in 2005 the ratio is likely to be one priest to every 2,200 of the faithful. The picture is bleak from whatever angle it is studied.[3]

The Catholic birth rate. Catholics and American families in general are having fewer children. The average number of children in a U.S. family in 1998 was 1.85.[4] The average number of children in a Catholic family was approximately the same. With two children or less in the typical Catholic household, most families will likely have but one son. Concern for the family name and the anticipation of the joy and comfort of grandchildren, it would seem, have dampened the encouragement and support parents might give to a son expressing interest in the priesthood. A quick poll of the college and theologate seminarians in my own diocese revealed that the average seminarian had three siblings. Vocations to the priesthood, it appears, tend to come from Catholic families with four or more children. When the high divorce rate, approaching 50 percent in many areas of the country, is factored in, the number of traditional Catholic families with more than two children is significantly reduced.

Catholic social and economic success. Vocations to the priesthood and religious life were plentiful when the U.S. Catholic Church was mostly immigrant and ethnic. A strong Catholic subculture provided security and assistance to first generation families striving for a foothold in a new world that was both suspicious and often hostile to Catholic newcomers. In the working-class neighborhoods where most Catholics

[3]U.S. Bureau of the Census. FM-3. Average Number of Own Children under 18 per Family, by Type of Family, Internet release date: December 11, 1998.

[4]U.S. Bureau of the Census, Current Population Reports, P20-515 "Household and Family Characteristics: March 1998."

lived, the priest was often the best educated member of his family *and* the community, enjoyed considerable status and influence, and experienced a standard of living—sometimes including a housekeeper, laundress, and cook—few of his siblings or friends were yet to achieve. In the Catholic world of the early and middle twentieth century, the priest, without owning even an acre of land, belonged to the Catholic equivalent of a "landed-gentry." Where else could working class sons, after six or eight years of seminary, come to enjoy the benefits of household servants? Some of these factors appear to be at play in the burgeoning number of vocations coming from countries in Africa and Asia.

While Catholics still claim and celebrate their ethnic roots, they are now third, fourth, and fifth generation and far less likely to think of themselves as hyphenated Americans. After the G.I. Bill opened university doors to working-class Catholics, their own work ethic and ambition took over. Today they are among the best educated social-religious groups in the U.S. Catholics are often more than proportionately represented among CEOs, the academic and research elite, government agency leaders, the leadership levels of organized labor, and the higher levels of the safety forces. Their place in the arts, medicine, judiciary, law, and the information-technical fields is more than significant. The proliferation of vocational choices brought about by such economic, social, and professional success can be daunting to a young man considering a life commitment to the Church. So many paths lie open to him, paths that he can realistically follow with a high probability of success, that the stirrings of a call to the priesthood may simply go unheeded.

Clergy misconduct with minors. No one, of course, can gauge what the long-term impact of abuse by priests on minors will have on young men considering the priesthood and on their parents. It would be naïve, nevertheless, to assume it will be minimal. Candidates for the priesthood and their parents who know the Church's history should be able to put the sexual abuse crisis into perspective. Yet the numerous "dark ages" of the Church and priesthood's past do not have the existential impact and shock of the present crisis. Reflecting on the abuse crisis, the candidate wonders "just how healthy is this fraternity, this company of men, that I am considering joining?" And more than a few of these young men have suffered sexual overtures themselves by their parish priest—overtures they are less likely to brush off in the present climate.

A former Kansas City–St. Joseph vicar general, Fr. Norman Rotert, a priest for forty-two years, spoke with considerable candor at a 1995 luncheon talk to the Catholic Press Association:

> The shortage of priests is not going to be solved by gritting our teeth and praying for more vocations. Women are the ones who identify and nurture vocations, and they are not doing it anymore, and they are not going to do it, and all the preaching in the world is not going to change their minds. If you don't believe me, talk to them. I've interviewed them. They say, "A church that won't accept my daughters isn't going to get my son." "I know my son has a vocation to the priesthood but he won't accept celibacy." "I don't want my sons to go through what you and other priests have had to go through since the pedophilia issue surfaced."[5]

Rotert's candid remarks reminded me of a conversation with a priest colleague who, like most of us on the seminary faculty, did supply work on weekends. After Mass one Sunday, a young man approached him and said he might be interested in the priesthood. Apparently prepared for just such a moment, the priest handed him some vocation materials. Suddenly his mother stood between them and grabbed the pamphlet from her son's hand. Throwing it down, she said with a voice of steel, "No son of mine is going to be a damn priest." Perhaps surprised at her own vehemence, she added, "Nothing against you, Father. It's just that no son of mine is going to be a priest."

This kind of anger isn't often evident to priests greeting people after Eucharist on Sunday mornings, but it is there nonetheless. It matters little whether priests feel it is unfair and unwarranted, whether it's displaced or disproportionate. This mother's angry response falls into context, however, when viewed in light of a recent Cara report sponsored by the National Conference of Catholic Bishops. When asked to react to the statement: "You would encourage your child to pursue a career as priest or nun," parents' responses fell into the following four categories: *Agree:* 25 percent; *Strongly agree:* 8 percent; *Disagree:* 48 percent; and *Strongly disagree:* 19 percent. A staggering 67 percent disagreed or strongly disagreed with the statement. Only 33 percent agreed or strongly agreed. The angry mother in question apparently has a good deal of company. In light of this report, one in five Catholic parents would strongly resist a child pursuing a vocation to the priesthood or religious life. Evidence that two-thirds would withhold encouragement to a son or daughter considering a vocation underscores the challenge facing vocation directors and seminary recruiters. It also reveals an important factor in the vocation crisis that is regularly overlooked. Catholics, in stark contrast to parents of pre-

[5]Thomas C. Fox, "Journalists Hear Frank Talk About Church Issues," *National Catholic Reporter* (October 13, 1995) 2.

vious generations, are no longer likely to see priesthood and religious life as a healthy way of life for their children.

Near the end of Rotert's Catholic Press Association talk, he summarized the forces alienating Catholic parents and Catholics in general:

> The paternalistic attitudes, the increasing consciousness of women, the lack of appreciation for the value of celibacy, the large percentage of gay priests, the pedophilia crisis, all have so impacted our vocation recruitment efforts that I see no possibility of salvaging the priesthood as we know it today. We must talk about the issue if we are going to find a creative solution. Non-ordained lay pastors, closing parishes, twinning parishes are all temporary, stopgap measures. We are a sacramental church. We must celebrate the Eucharist or we will die.[6]

The Gay Crisis

We return to this perplexing issue in order to assess its impact on the present dearth of seminarians preparing for the priesthood. That a connection exists was highlighted by a remark a well-qualified candidate made to me shortly after deciding not to pursue seminary studies. He said he was seriously thinking of the priesthood until he became aware of the homosexuality issue in seminaries. That this issue alone could dissuade a man from pursuing studies leading to the priesthood underscores its significance.

Gay seminarians are likely to feel at home and at ease in a seminary with a significant gay population. They feel they belong and their need for meaningful, deep relationships with other gay men is easily met, and because they instinctively recognize other gay seminarians, circles of support and camaraderie are quickly formed. Their nurturing community provides engaging conversation reflecting their common interests in spirituality and the performing arts. Not infrequently, however, the sexual contacts and romantic unions among gay seminarians creates intense and complicated webs of intrigue and jealousy leading to considerable inner conflict. Here the sexually ambiguous seminarian drawn into the gay subculture is particularly at risk. The straight seminarian, meanwhile, feels out of place and may interpret his inner destabilization as a sign that he does not have a vocation to the priesthood.

The Authority Crisis

Priests clearly have taken it on the chin in the last quarter of the twentieth century. The blows have echoed throughout the Catholic

[6]Ibid.

community as well as to the outposts of the global village. Priests and their foibles have been fodder for the op/ed pages of our newspapers and ripe material for cartoonists, satirists, and comedians. Perhaps the priest-pedophile jokes, even more than the painful media coverage, signaled the extent of the clerical free-fall from grace. Another fall, however, was taking place during the clergy misconduct-with-minors crisis. And while it equally threatened the welfare and mission of the Church, it had none of the tabloid features necessary to guarantee the same widespread attention in the secular media.

As church leadership faced the stress and tension of crisis management brought on by a small but significant number of its priests, the Church's teaching office saw its power to enlighten and reconcile, to challenge and encourage, diminished by its unwillingness to listen seriously to those outside the inner corridors of the Vatican establishment, including large numbers of bishops belonging to the very college constituted to teach authoritatively in the name of Christ.

If priests lost a good deal of the status and respect won for them by the presbyters who had gone before them, bishops lost a good deal of their credibility. In the summer of 1995, approximately forty U.S. bishops submitted a document to the leaders of the National Conference of Catholic Bishops calling for a more effective structure for dialogue with Rome. The document notes that

> We [the U.S. bishops] have taken major and commendable steps to make it possible for people to hear through the media what we have to say at meetings. We now need to take steps to be sure that we hear what the people have to say to us. . . . We are teachers, but teachers have to be good listeners. . . . Catholic bishops experience a credibility problem with many faithful people. There are vast numbers of "Sunday only" Catholics or, worse, Catholics in name only. We have succeeded in instructing Catholics in the basic truths, laws and practices of the church, but not in handing on our relationship in faith to a loving God.[7]

Many educated laity lost confidence in moral teachings heard as assertions and supported primarily by the Church's claim that its teachings were sufficiently undergirded by biblical and theological sources.[8] Practicing Catholics, in large numbers, simply bracketed policies and lower-level church teachings that didn't square with their experience. There was no challenge to core gospel teachings or revealed dogmas, but in significant patterns of collective discernment

---

[7] *National Catholic Reporter* (June 30, 1995) 3 and 28.

[8] See Dean R. Hoge, "Catholic Generations Polarized On Gender and Sex," *America* (November 21, 1998) 16–18.

they simply didn't take every church pronouncement as something to be unquestionably accepted. Especially in matters of sexuality, the Church's teaching fell on deaf ears. Not only did the majority of Catholics not believe that every intentional sexual fantasy was seriously sinful, they seemed to approach once-taboo issues for Catholics, such as living together before marriage, with considerable forbearance. Missing Mass on Sunday, while remaining an "ought" for most Catholics, no longer carried the threat of eternal damnation. To be sure, the "under pain of mortal sin" threat concerning relatively lesser matters (eating meat on Fridays, missing Mass on a given Sunday, for example) was used in order to underscore practices of virtue and responsibility that were deemed necessary for salvation. Yet, instructing the People of God that they must do something, or refrain from doing something, because non-compliance was mortally sinful no longer brought about the desired effect.

The post-conciliar Catholic imagination understood the mercy and judgment of God in a different light. Sadly, in matters of profound significance—the dignity of human life, the evil of war, wanton violence, systemic injustice, spiritual suffocation from materialism and consumerism—the liberating light and wisdom of the Church's teaching authority was readily ignored or precipitously dismissed.

Caught in the wake of the Church's authority crisis, priests have seen their moral authority, their ability to lead and to offer pastoral guidance, likewise diminished. The sins and crimes of some of their brother priests and bishops, of course, contributed in no small measure to the weakening of their authority. The scandal of clergy misconduct with minors has cast a long shadow on the credibility and authority of priests and bishops—a shadow that will last well into the twenty-first century. They are still welcomed as pastoral caregivers, of course, but their prophetic preaching of the gospel message is taken by many with a grain of salt. Still welcomed as "chaplains" to comfort and console, they are less likely to be welcomed as pastors who bear a word from the Lord. While it is clear that many bishops and priests are indeed credible and compelling teachers both to Catholics and to society at large, the crisis of credibility and authority shows no signs of abating.

Denis Hurley, the late archbishop of Durban, acknowledged by John Tracy Ellis as "one of the relatively few prophetic figures among the English-speaking hierarchies of the world,"[9] acknowledged the

---

[9]John Tracy Ellis, "Whence Did They Come, These Uncertain Priests of the 1960's," *American Ecclesiastical Review*, vol. 162, no. 3 (March 1970) 158–59.

challenge facing church authority and proposed a new model for exercising it:

> There is no going back to the old idea that ready-made solutions can be handed down by authority. Authority's function is to set up the conditions in which a solution can be sought by the Church, that is, the community. In most cases there will be no final solution, only a continual attempt to adjust to a perpetually evolving situation.[10]

In a pastoral letter criticizing the 1997 *Instruction on Certain Questions Regarding the Collaboration of the Non-ordained Faithful in the Sacred Ministry of Priests,* signed by the heads of eight Vatican offices, Bishop Reinhold Stecher of Innsbruck addressed the issue of authority. He argued that the decree was concerned entirely with defending the rights of the ordained, missing the urgent problem of Catholic communities without regular celebrations of Eucharist:

> For some time now we have been offering people, tacitly but in reality, a non-sacramental way of salvation. . . . The difficulty arises because instead of making provision for the Eucharist based on the spiritual health of the Christian community we concentrate on purely human laws about who is authorized to do what—laws which ignore God's will that all should be saved as well as the essentially eucharistic structure of the community. Everything is sacrificed to a definition of church office for which there is no basis in revelation.[11]

Stecher reports a telling conversation with another bishop that left him exasperated. He follows with a commentary both prophetic and disturbing.

> Not long ago a bishop renowned for his conservatism said to me with a smile: "In our diocese every priest has three parishes—and things run splendidly." That most reverend gentleman has never had the responsibility for even one parish—let alone three. If he had, he could hardly have made such a lighthearted remark. In France I have met worn-out, exhausted priests who have to attend to seven or even ten parishes. Even if such priests have the best theological qualifications, their voices will never be heard in the Church's higher councils. Such priests are not made bishops. Few bishops know what these priests face—with the result that their experiences and frustrations are never represented at the Church's highest level. The best we bishops can do is to sigh sympa-

---

[10] Introduction to *The Experiences of the Priesthood*, ed. Brian Passman (Wilkes-Barre, Pa.: Dimension Books, 1968) xvi.

[11] Reinhold Stecher, "Challenge to the Church," *The Tablet* (December 20–27, 1997) 1668.

thetically about the difficulties our priests face and utter moving complaints about the shortage of Christian families capable of producing
celibate vocations. At a higher level still all energies are devoted to defending the existing rules—as in this latest decree. The Church's real
needs are never considered. . . . The tendency to place human laws
and traditions above our divine commission is the most shocking aspect
of many church decisions at the end of this millennium.[12]

Stecher's candid letter underscores in bold strokes the frustration
and discouragement many priests feel as they encounter resistance to
dialogue and the practice of true collegiality. Certain that their voice
is not taken seriously, morale remains low. Preaching, in this climate,
particularly wears on priests' souls. Only a deep and integrated spirituality grounded in hard thinking and study offers any hope for successfully tending God's word to a people hungry for gospel freedom
and holiness.[13]

The Intellectual Crisis

One of the effects of the dramatic decline in the number of priests
during the last three decades of the twentieth century has received relatively little attention—the impact on the intellectual lives of clergy.
Fewer priests have led to longer working days for most of them. Often
responsible for more than one parish, they tend to spend more time on
the road. At the end of the day, there may be precious little psychic energy for literature, theology, and Scripture—essential for priming the
sacramental imagination so critical for effective preaching. When the intellectual life of the priest grows shallow, his preaching inevitably suffers,
and when his preaching is poor, there is precious little affirmation.
Priests who preach well are regularly affirmed. Priests who don't, aren't.

Clergy, I believe, are no more in need of affirmation than most
people, but being human, it can sustain them in times of fatigue and
discouragement. The life of the mind is important for other reasons
as well. Serious reading and study is intimately connected with the life
of the spirit. The inner life of the priest who is determined to feed his
mind is simply different from the inner life of the priest who doesn't.
There is a different quality to his prayer and contemplation, and his

---

[12]Ibid.

[13]See *The Spirituality of the Diocesan Priest*, ed. Donald B. Cozzens (Collegeville:
The Liturgical Press, 1997) for a collection of essays addressing the spirituality of the
parish priest. See also Robert M. Schwartz, *Servant Leaders of the People of God* (New
York: Paulist Press, 1989).

prayerful living permits glimpses into the mostly hidden drama of grace at play in the ordinary events of life.[14]

Without regular study and serious reading, clergy easily come under the influence of the polar opposites of relativism and fundamentalism.[15] Although relatively few priests are shaped to any significant degree by the relativism of our age, a number might be described as "soft liberals," uncritically open to current trends of thought raised up in a culture wary of dogmatic and doctrinal pronouncements.

The greater danger for priests appears to be an ecclesial fundamentalism, which, according to the Master of the Dominican Order, Timothy Radcliffe,

> derives from a profound fear of thinking, and which offers *the false hope of faith without ambiguity*. Within the Church this fundamentalism sometimes takes the form of an unthinking repetition of received words, a refusal to take part in the never ending search for understanding, an intolerance of all for whom tradition is not just a revelation but also an invitation to draw nearer to mystery.

Radcliffe continues:

> This fundamentalism may appear to be a rocklike fidelity to orthodoxy, but it contradicts a fundamental principle of our faith, which is that when we argue and reason we honour our Creator and Redeemer who gave us minds with which to think and to draw near to Him.[16]

Saturated and shaken by the radical individualism and relativism of contemporary society, priests and seminarians may be tempted to eschew the anxiety inherent in such a society by embracing an ecclesial fundamentalism that, in their eyes, is nothing other than strict orthodoxy. At the same time, they have little tolerance for the ambiguous dimension to all knowledge that is communicated by the symbols we call language.

---

[14]See Eugene Hemrick, "An Aggiornamento for Seminary Formation," *Seminary Journal,* vol. 1, no. 2 (Fall 1995) 40–50. Hemrick writes:
> (Effective priests) reflect healthy spiritual-intellectual vitality. They are critical thinkers who model modern-day virtues, love the Eucharist, and use biblical images to define their ministry. They cherish the inspiration they receive from the faith of those they serve, and marvel at the awesomeness of unexpected religious experiences (40).

[15]See Timothy Radcliffe, O.P., "The Wellspring of Hope—Study and the Annunciation of the Good News," *International Dominican Information,* no. 337 (January 1996) especially 5–6. Radcliffe's masterful treatment of these two pitfalls deserves careful study.

[16]Ibid., 6.

It bears repeating that priests who study regularly, pray differently. Their reading and reflection become staples of their spiritual lives allowing their imaginations to encounter with ever fresh insight the mysterious presence of God. Their preaching echoes the passion and liberating force of the Word made flesh in the present assembly. Having discovered the narrative nature of God's revelation and the human psyche, they listen for *rumors of angels* in the stories of love and betrayal, of comedy and tragedy, spoken by their parishioners. Strangely, the loneliness inherent to celibate ministry takes on a different hue. Having fed their minds and hearts with the wisdom of the ancients and the insights of contemporary theologians and spiritual writers, they discover a certain intimacy of soul in their hours of solitude. Such liberating and purifying study must be engaged, of course, as an act of faith and prayer.[17] Priests who study in order to win arguments and change people's minds simply know more facts than when they opened their book. Approaching study without a sense of reverence and humility leads to pride and hardness of heart.

There remains a significant number of priests who lead vibrant intellectual lives whose vigor and discipline would receive an approving nod from the late John Tracy Ellis. Some pursue formal post-seminary studies leading to advanced degrees. Others take summer courses and attend seminars and workshops that sharpen their ministry skills and expand their intellectual horizons. Countless others read widely and wisely, developing personal libraries that nourish their imaginations and souls. The quality of mind and soul of these men enriches the presbyterate and the congregations they serve. These are the priests who will sustain their colleagues through the present years of crisis; it is their voices that will speak the collective wisdom of the fraternity of presbyters. Their commitment to prayer, study, and ministry will continue to change the face of the priesthood well into the twenty-first century.

Conclusion

While only the naïve or disingenuous would argue that the crises facing the priesthood are simply passing blips on the Church's ever-illuminated screen, there are signs of hope on the horizon. The first of these signs is the growing number of priests who believe the present critical problems must be forthrightly faced. Joined with bishops and laity who see the Spirit at work in the People of God, priests

---

[17]See Simone Weil, *Waiting for God* (New York: Harper Colophon Books, 1951) especially the essay, "Reflections on the Right Use of School Studies with a View to the Love of God."

will begin to speak what their pastoral experience and theological reflection require them to speak. Having listened long and hard to their parishioners and to their own inner voices, they are ready for respectful, meaningful dialogue with their ecclesial superiors. The passivity evident in numerous priests is ready it seems to give way to committed, responsible action to address the underlying causes of the present troubled situation. They will face criticism, of course, from those who see any attempt to address the issues and concerns outlined above as threatening to the very well-being and integrity of the Church. John Tracy Ellis appreciated the risk involved here. During an address to the Association of Chicago priests in 1968, he said:

> What I find particularly disappointing and even depressing, however, . . . is that while numerous priests are quite articulate in private about the unhappiness they feel with their present lot, they will not take the steps to improve it even when offered an opportunity through approved channels such as committees of their diocesan senates. One gets the impression that they would prefer not to be confronted with the consequences that such a free action often entails. In a word, they would seem to fall into that category of man about whom Sir Isaiah Berlin was talking when he said, "Where there is no choice, there is no anxiety; and a happy release from responsibility."[18]

Another reason for hope lies in the apparent purification and maturation the priesthood has undergone in the last two decades of the twentieth century. From their own pastoral experience, priests know that something happens to the soul when it is subjected to ordeal upon ordeal, to unrelenting criticism, and to the anxiety that follows the loss of one's place and identity. Either it surrenders to despair or chooses to hope against hope that life will go on, that mercy upon mercy will lift it up. Most priests have not given in to despair or lost their nerve. Their confidence has been shaken, to be sure, and their spirit bruised. But now, with status diminished and reputation questioned, priests have turned with renewed poverty of soul to the sus-

---

[18]The address, in abridged form, was published in *The American Ecclesiastical Review,* vol. 162, no. 3 (March 1970) 145–72. For an example of a priest with the courage to speak about his experience of the Church and priesthood see Tony Flannery, *From the Inside: A Priest's View of the Catholic Church* (Dublin: Mercier Press, 1999). Flannery writes: "At various times throughout my life in the Church I have known it to be authoritarian, dogmatic, devious, sef-seeking and even on occasion corrupt. But it has also opened up for me a world of great depth and beauty; it has been a gateway to mystery and to the realm of the spirit. I have experienced kindness, support and encouragement" (7).

taining mercy and grace of God. In the midst of unprecedented crises, they stand as men without illusions, totally dependent on the strength of the Spirit. In the truth of their circumstances, their humility inspires freedom and courage.

The strongest reason for hope, of course, is their faith in the power of the Spirit to be with them through the darkest hours. In the power of the Spirit they are reminded that nothing can separate them from Christ's abiding love and the saving promise of their creator God. In this abiding love and saving promise they look, without fear, to the renewal and transformation of the priesthood. Behind the changing face of the priesthood remains the saving face of Jesus the Christ.

Index